Preschool Skills

AF700894

Best Value Books

Table Of Contents

The student pages in this book have been specially prepared for reproduction on any standard copying machine.

Permission is hereby granted to the purchaser of this book to reproduce student pages for classroom use only. Reproduction for commercial resale or for an entire school or school system is strictly prohibited. No part of this book may be reproduced for storage in a retrieval system, or transmitted in any form, by any means (electronic, recording, mechanical, or otherwise) without the prior written permission of the publisher.

Kelley Wingate products are available at fine educational supply stores throughout the U. S. and Canada.

Preschool Skills **CD-3702** Printed in the United States Of America ISBN 0-88724-420-3

Ready-To-Use Ideas and Activities

This book was developed to help children master basic readiness skills. These skills are fundamental in helping children become successful learners.

Remember as you read through the activities listed below, that all children learn at their own rate. Although repetition is important, it is critical to build self-esteem and self-confidence in children in order to help them become successful.

If you are working with a child at home, try to set up a quiet comfortable environment where you will work. Make it a special time to which you each look forward. Do only a few activities at a time. Try to end each session on a positive note,and remember that fostering self-confidence and self-esteem are critical to the learning process.

The following activities are meant to be used as follow up ideas or enrichment activities to supplement the ones in this book.

Tracing is a wonderful way for children to work on fine motor skills. Dot-to-dot books provide an excellent opportunity for children to work on fine motor as well as sequencing skills. Another way to work on tracing skills at home is with a salt box. Take the top of a shoe box. Cut out a few pieces of paper to fit in the box top. Take a thick black marker and draw a variety of wavy and or curvy lines. Put a thin layer of salt over the paper. Let the children trace the lines through the salt. Children will get a wonderful tactile sense of what they are doing by tracing in the salt.

It is also fun to follow the lines outdoors. Take a piece of sidewalk chalk and draw wavy and curly lines down the sidewalk or on the playground. Let children try to walk on the line. Have them try to walk on the line in very small steps, or even walk heel to toe if they can.

Cutting activities: Beginning scissor skills can be hard to master. Obviously the best way to master scissors skills is to practice. Try taking blank paper and drawing shapes for children to cut out with thick markers so they can try to stay in the marker line. Begin by just drawing a single right angle like a large capital "L" and let the children cut on the straight lines. Let them keep doing it until

©1995 Kelley Wingate Publications, Inc.

Ready-To-Use Ideas and Activities

they have mastered it. Once they have mastered a right angle try curves, again drawn with thick marker lines which they can cut through. Next try basic shapes like a square, circle, oval, and triangle.

As children become more adept at cutting, let them try cutting on a variety materials other that paper such as, fabric, felt, cardboard, aluminum foil, or paper bags.

The back of this book has removable flash cards. Pull the flash cards out and either cut them apart or, if you have access to a paper cutter, use that to cut the flash cards apart. The flash cards are designed to help reinforce many of the basic skills children must learn like the alphabet, colors, shapes, and numbers. The activities listed below have proven themselves successful in learning these basic skills. They are also open ended enough that children will discover new information by continuing to do them.

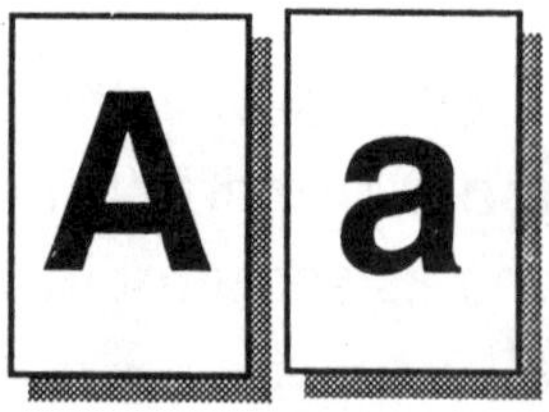

Take the twenty-six capital letter flash cards. Have children put them in alphabetical order. Take the lowercase alphabet flash cards and see if the children can put the correct lowercase letter under the corresponding capital letter. Talk about each of the letters and what sound they make. Turn over the capital letter and see what picture is on the other side. See how many other words the children can think of that start with that letter sound.

Another way to help reinforce the letters of the alphabet is by using a salt box. Take the capital letter flash cards and put a couple of them in the top of a shoebox or other shallow box. Put a light layer of salt over the inside of the box. Let the children trace over the letters through the salt. This is an excellent way for children to get a tactile feel for each of the letters.

Take both sets of number flash cards. Have the children put the numeric cards in order from 0 to 10. Next take the flash cards which have the numbers written out and see if the children can match the written number word with the numeric symbol. Once they can do that, try playing concentration by matching the number word to the numeral.

©1995 Kelley Wingate Publications, Inc.

Ready-To-Use Ideas and Activities

Children may want to trace over the numbers in a salt box in order to get tactile feel for each number. Salt boxes can be a good tool for reinforcing basic skills children are learning.

Put the number flash cards out in order. Take a bag of beans or a set of counters. See if the children can put the correct number of beans in front of each number card.

You may want to take the blank flash cards and make other number cards. For example make one that says "20" on it. See if the children can count to "20"and if they can count out the correct number of beans. Try "30", "40", and "50".

Take the color and shape flash cards. Take each "black and white" shape flash card one at a time, look at it, identify it, and talk about it. For example talk about the circle flash card. Where else do you see circles around you: coins, tires on cars, the sun, many knobs on TV's and other electronic equipment, etc. The oval is not as common, but you do see it in an egg or in a picture of how the earth rotates around the sun. Can the children think of any other shapes? There are some other really interesting shapes like a rhombus (an equilateral parallelogram), a pentagon, an octagon, a parallelogram, or a trapezoid.

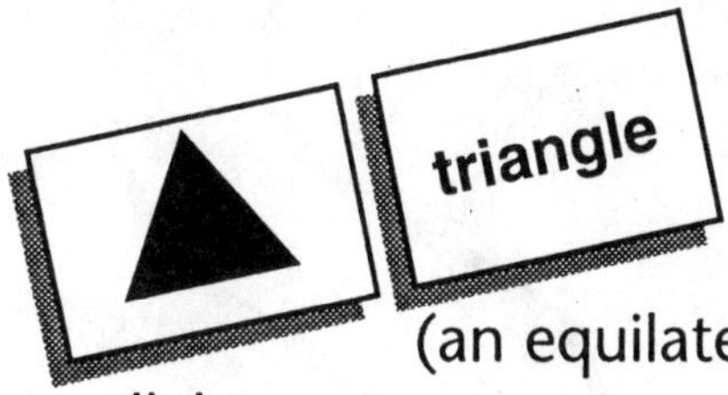

Take the set of colored shape flash cards and the black and white ones and see if the children can match the black and white shape to the correct colored shape. This could be a great way to start a discussion on attributes. For example, we have two cards that have squares on them. They are alike in that both are squares. They are different in that one is brown and the other is not.

Leave the black and white set of flash cards face up, and turn the colored set, which has the shape word written on them word side up. See if the children can sound out the shape word. Talk about the words and then see if they can match the word with the correct picture.

Name ____________________ Skill: Following a maze

Follow the maze to help the children find their pets.

©1995 Kelley Wingate Publications, Inc.

Name ______________________________ Skill: Following a maze

Follow the maze to help the mother bird get back to her nest.

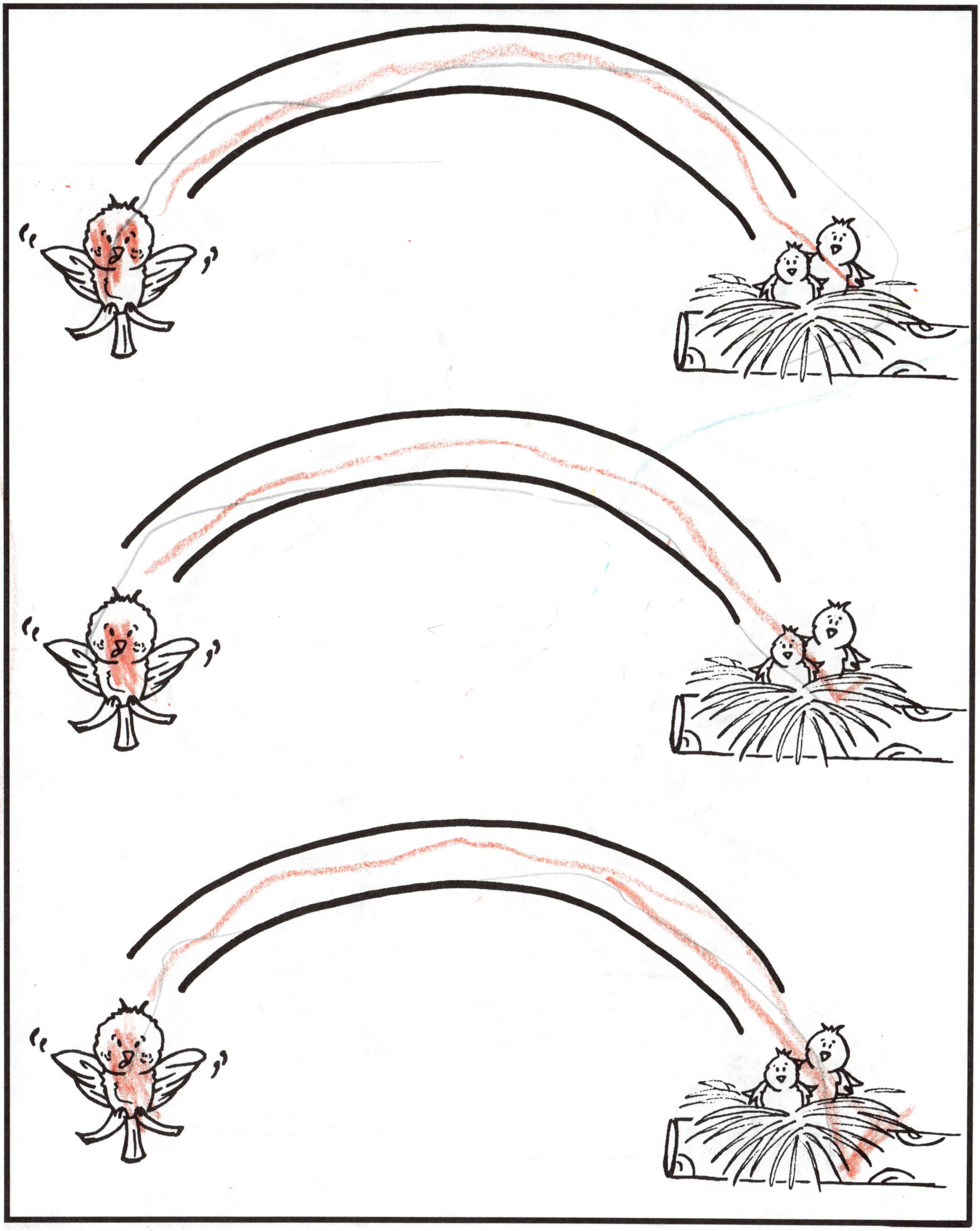

©1995 Kelley Wingate Publications, Inc.

Name ______________________________ Skill: Following a maze

Follow the maze to show each duck the way to the pond.

Name ________________________________ Skill: Following a maze

Follow the maze to help the car find some gas.

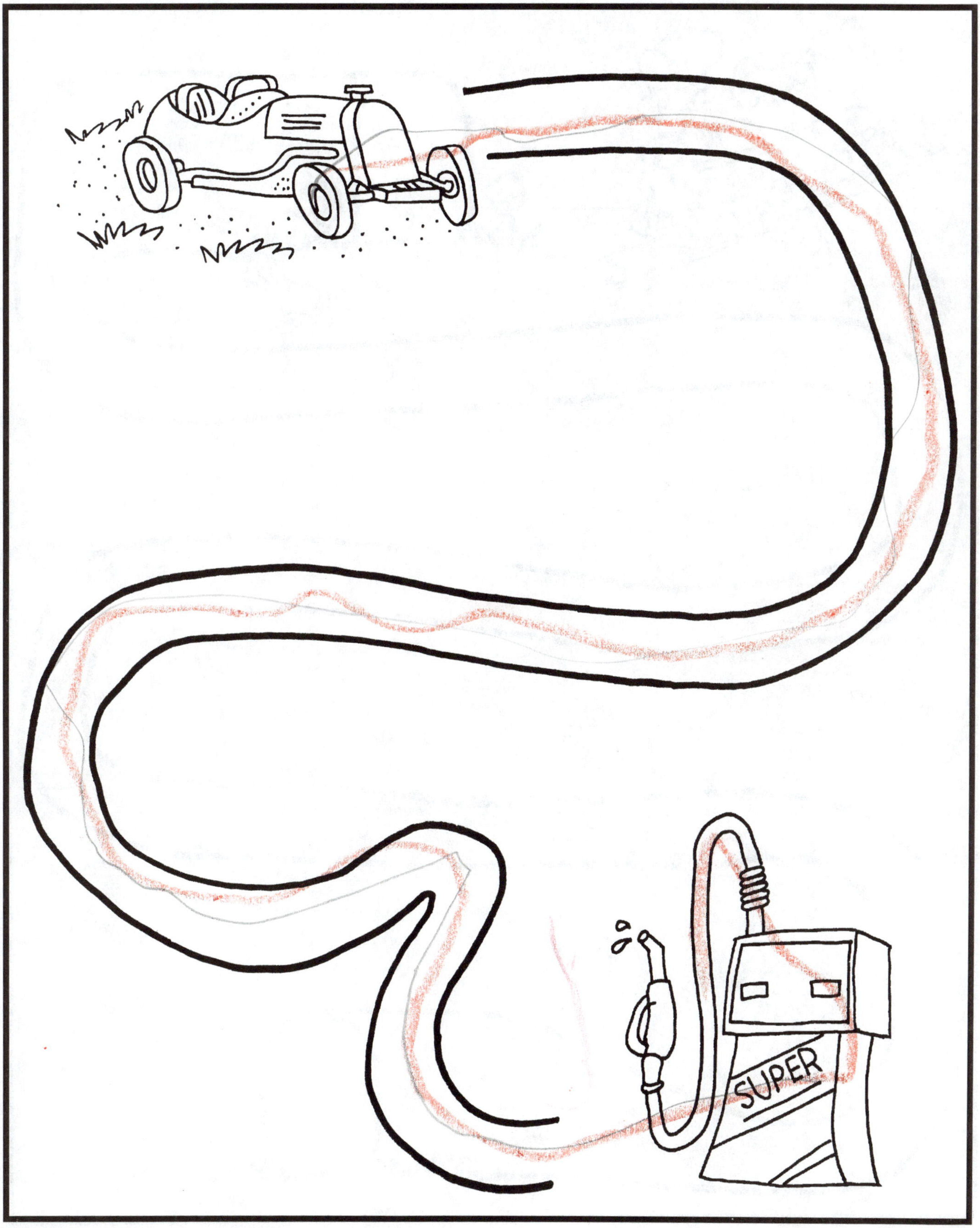

©1995 Kelley Wingate Publications, Inc.

Name ______________________________ Skill: Following a maze

Follow the maze to help the train get through the tunnel.

©1995 Kelley Wingate Publications, Inc.

Name ______________________________ Skill: Tracing straight lines

Trace over the path that the tractor must take to get to each corn field.

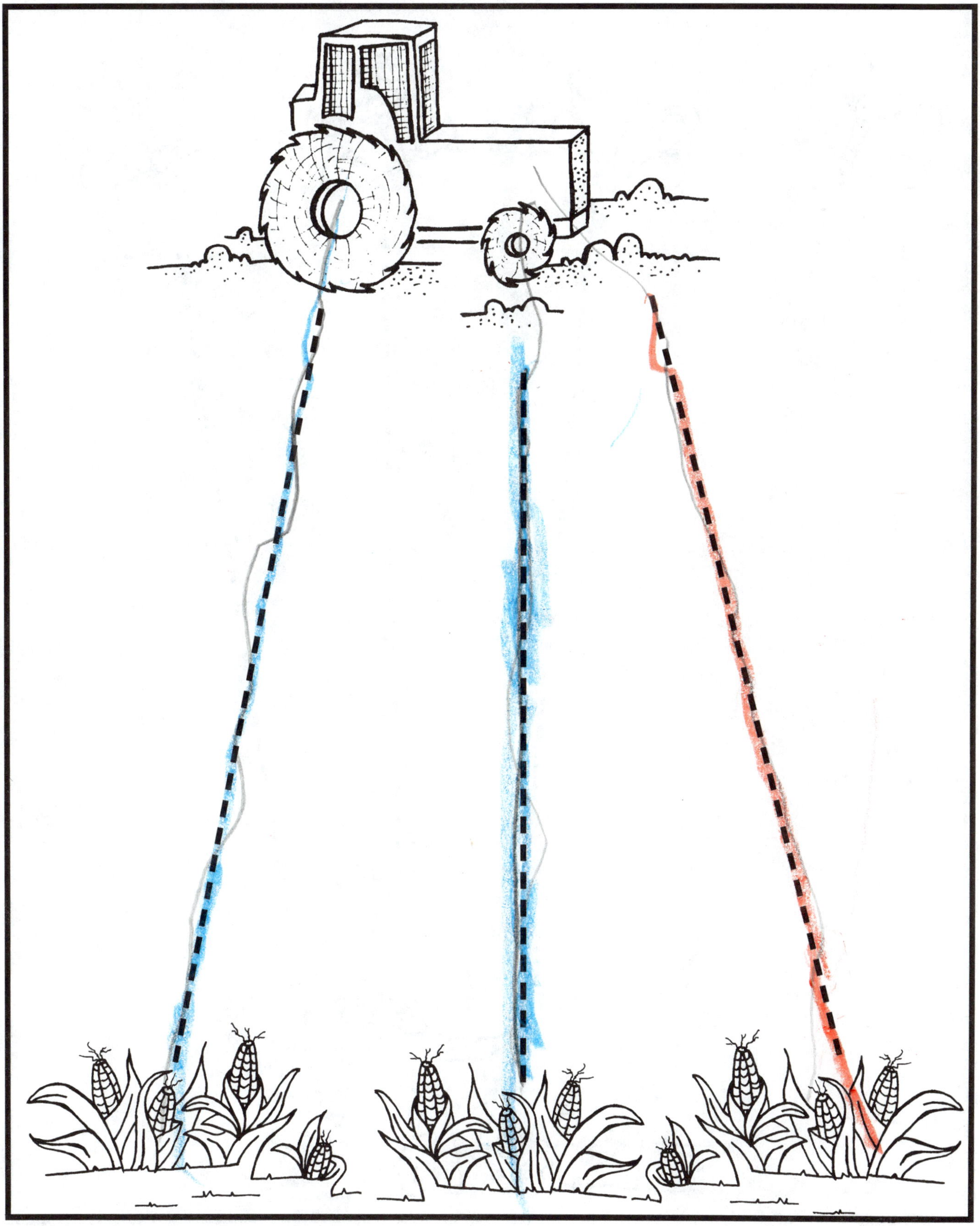

©1995 Kelley Wingate Publications, Inc.

Name ______________________ Skill: Tracing straight lines

Trace the path that each butterfly takes to get to the flowers.

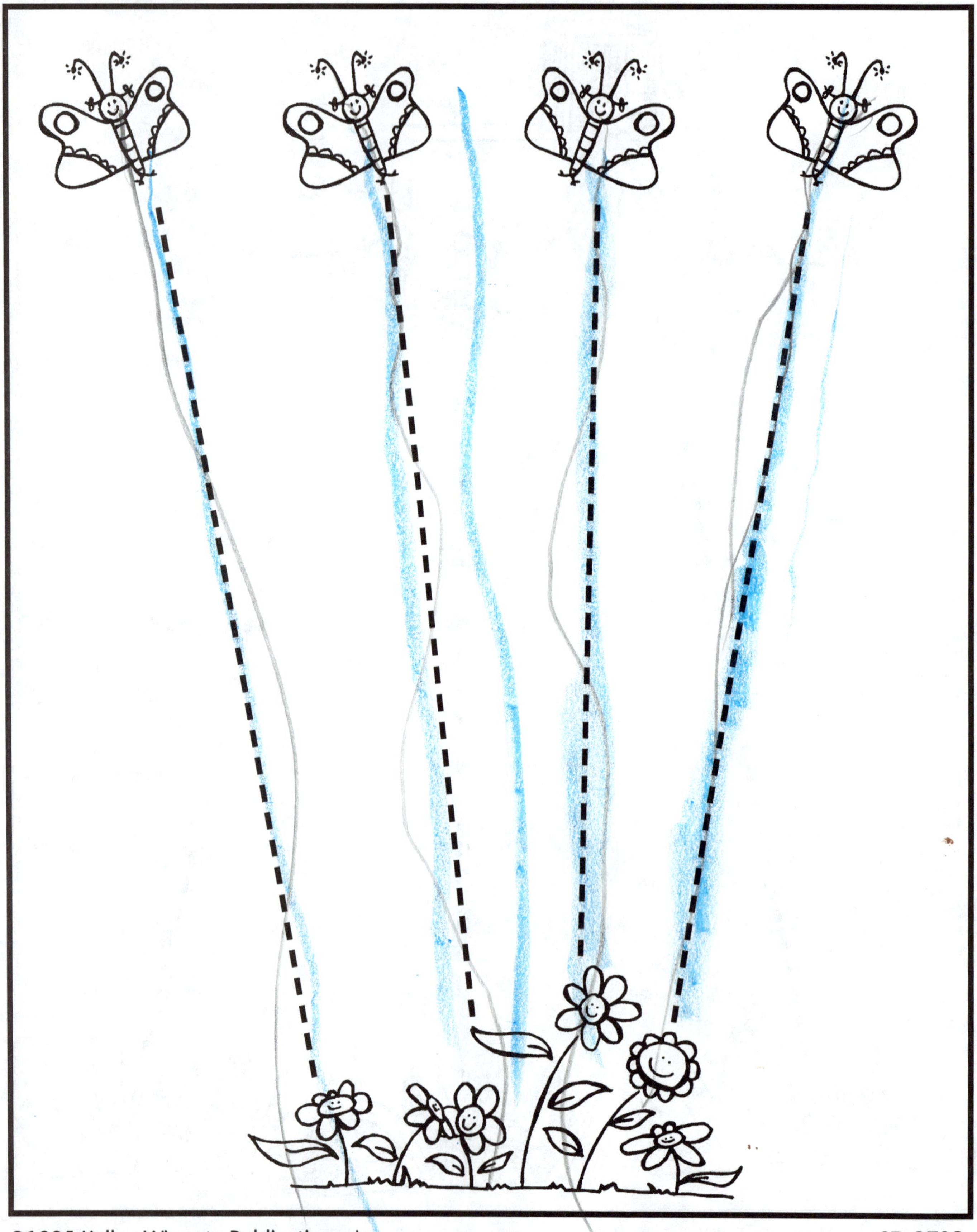

Name ______________________________ Skill: Tracing dotted lines

Trace over the dotted lines to help the turtles cross the streets.

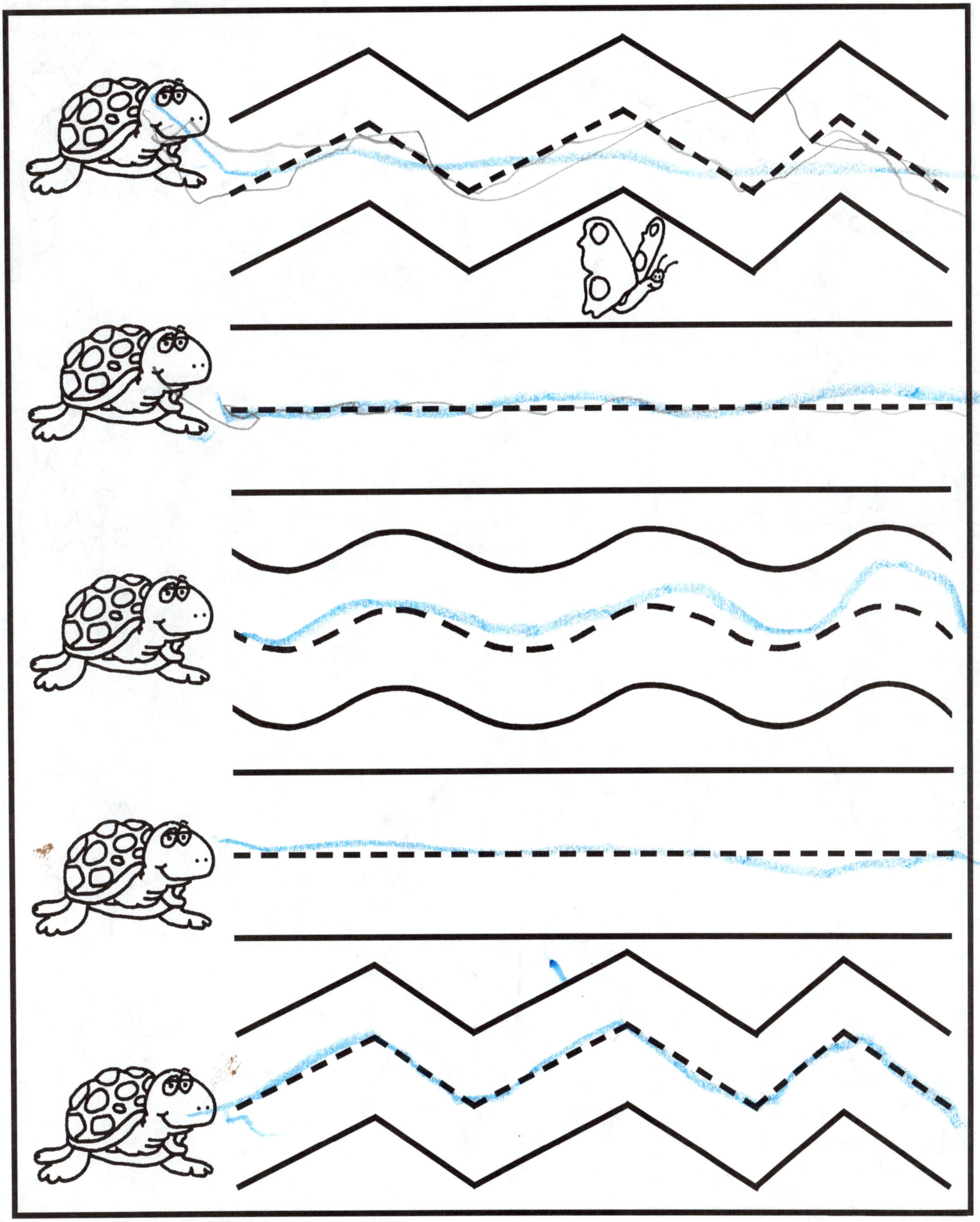

©1995 Kelley Wingate Publications, Inc.

Name ______________________________ Skill: Tracing curved lines

Trace over the dotted lines to hop each bunny to the carrots.

©1995 Kelley Wingate Publications, Inc.

Name ________________________________ Skill: Tracing curved lines

Trace over the dotted lines to complete the telephone cords.

Name ______________________ Skill: Tracing curved lines

Trace over the dotted lines to complete the sun and clouds. Draw your favorite bird on a cloud. Color the sun yellow.

Name ____ Skill: Tracing squares

Trace over the dotted lines to complete the squares.
Color each square a different color.

Name ______________________________ Skill: Tracing circles

Trace over the dotted lines to complete the gumballs.
Color each gumball a different color.

©1995 Kelley Wingate Publications, Inc.

Name ________________________________ Skill: Tracing triangles

Trace over the triangles to complete the butterflys.

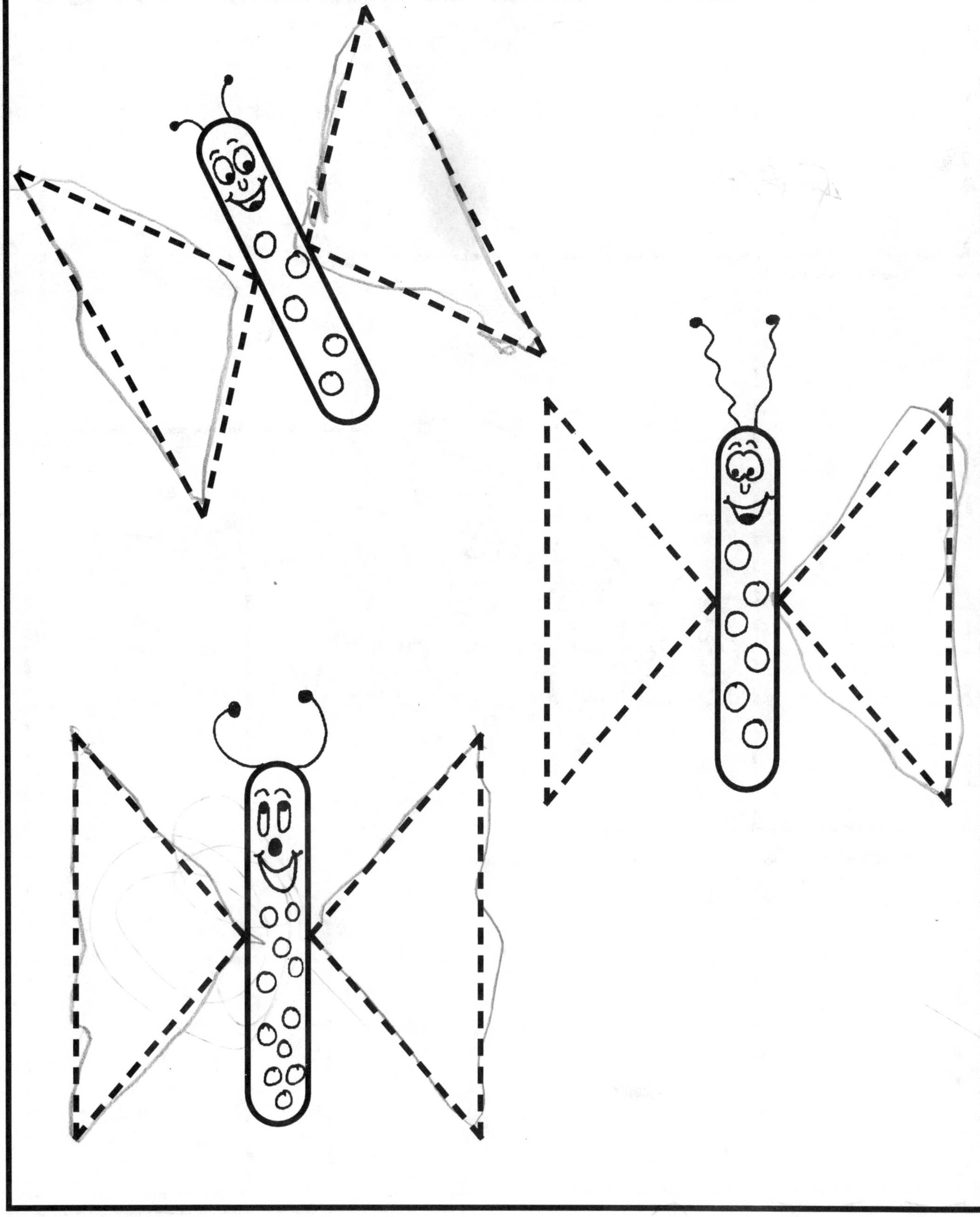

Name ______________________________ Skill: Tracing rectangles

Trace over the dotted lines to complete the rectangles.
Color two rectangles green. Color three rectangles orange.

©1995 Kelley Wingate Publications, Inc.

Name ______________________________ Skill: Tracing shapes

Trace over the dotted lines to complete the picture.
Color the completed picture.

©1995 Kelley Wingate Publications, Inc.

Name ______________________________ Skill: Tracing stars

Trace over the dotted lines to complete the stars.
Color the stars yellow.

©1995 Kelley Wingate Publications, Inc.

Name ______________________________ Skill: Tracing Ice cream cones

Trace over the dotted lines to complete the ice cream cones.
Color the ice cream the color of your favorite flavor.

©1995 Kelley Wingate Publications, Inc.

Name ______________________________ Skill: Tracing fish

Trace over the dotted lines to complete the fish.
Color the fish green.

©1995 Kelley Wingate Publications, Inc.

Name ______________________________ Skill: Tracing cars

Trace over the dotted lines to complete the cars.
Color each car a different color.

©1995 Kelley Wingate Publications, Inc.

Name ______________________________________ Skill: Cutting curved lines

✄ Cut the paths that lead to the castles.

©1995 Kelley Wingate Publications, Inc.

Name ______________________________ Skill: Cutting curved lines

✂ Cut the path that each car has made to get to the finish line.

©1995 Kelley Wingate Publications, Inc.

Name ______________________________ Skill: Cutting curved lines

✂ Cut the trails that each boat makes.

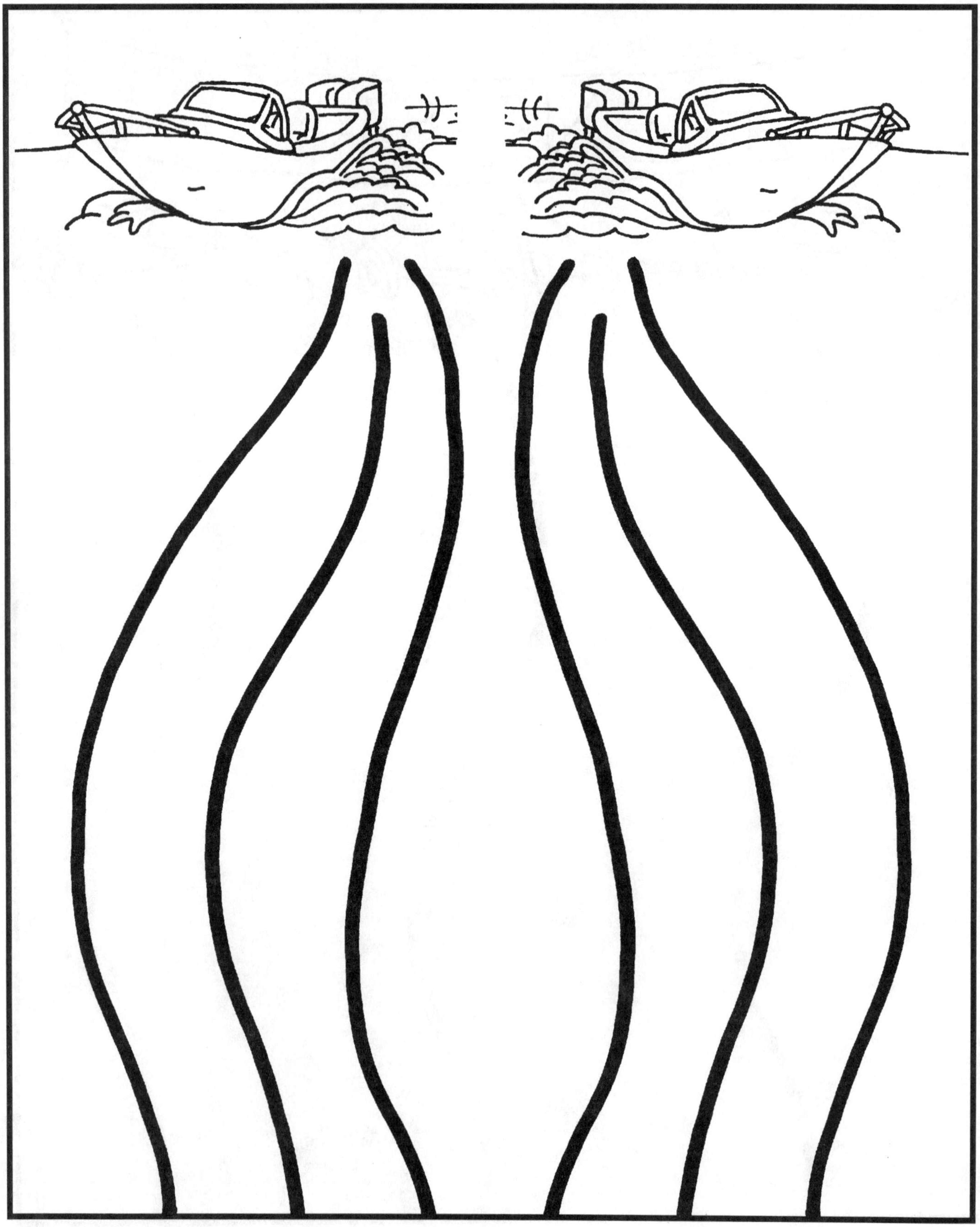

©1995 Kelley Wingate Publications, Inc.

Name ______________________________ Skill: Cutting cuved lines

✂ Cut the trail made by the blimp.

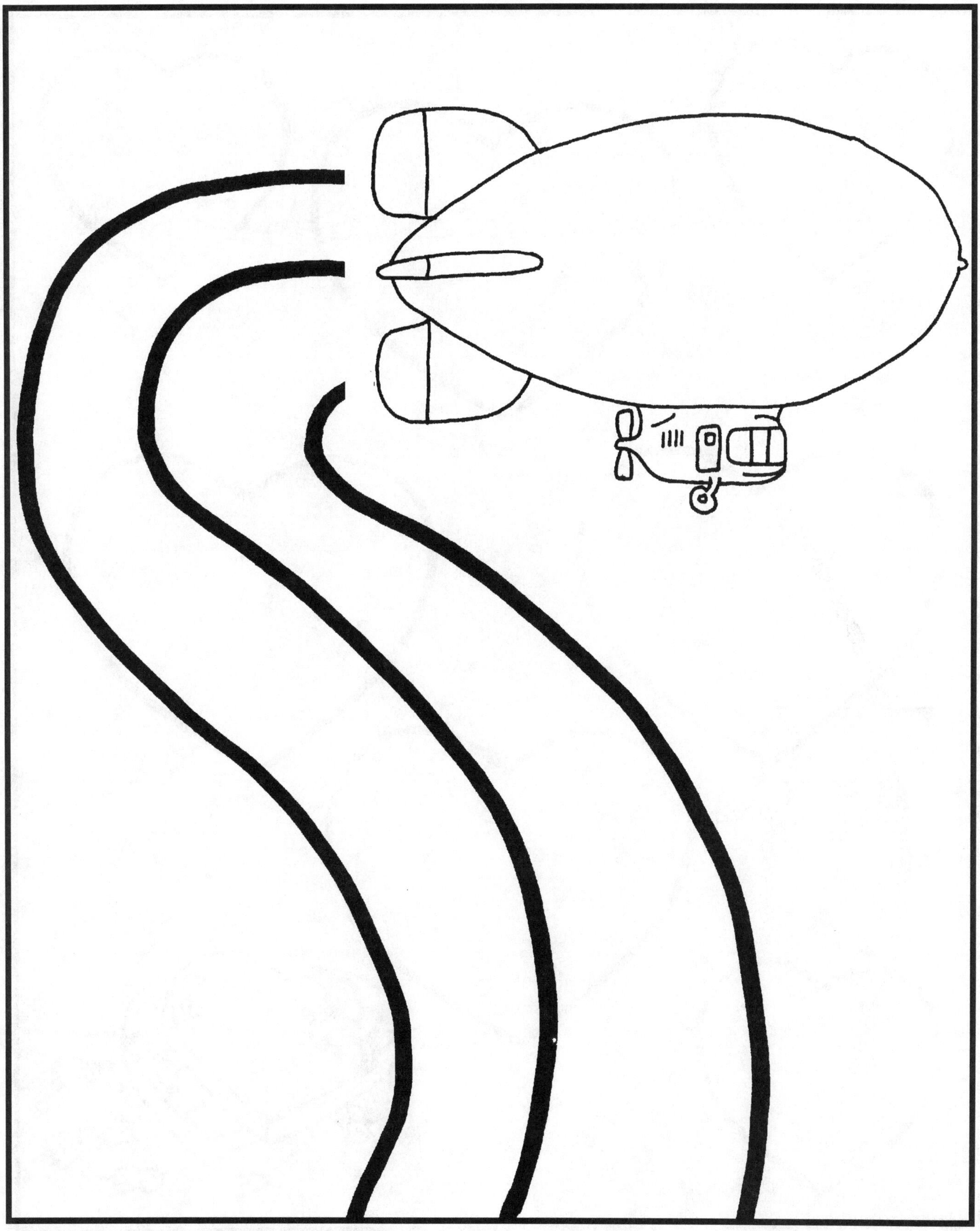

Name ______________________________ Skill: Cutting hearts

Color the big hearts red. Color the little hearts pink.

✂ Cut out the hearts.

©1995 Kelley Wingate Publications, Inc.

Name ____________________ Skill: Cutting stars

Color each star a different color.

✂ Cut out the stars.

Name ________________________________ Skill: Cutting straight lines

✂ Cut the path that the car takes to get home.

Name ____________________ Skill: Cutting leaves

Color two leaves orange. Color two leaves yellow.
Color two leaves brown. ✂ Cut out the leaves.

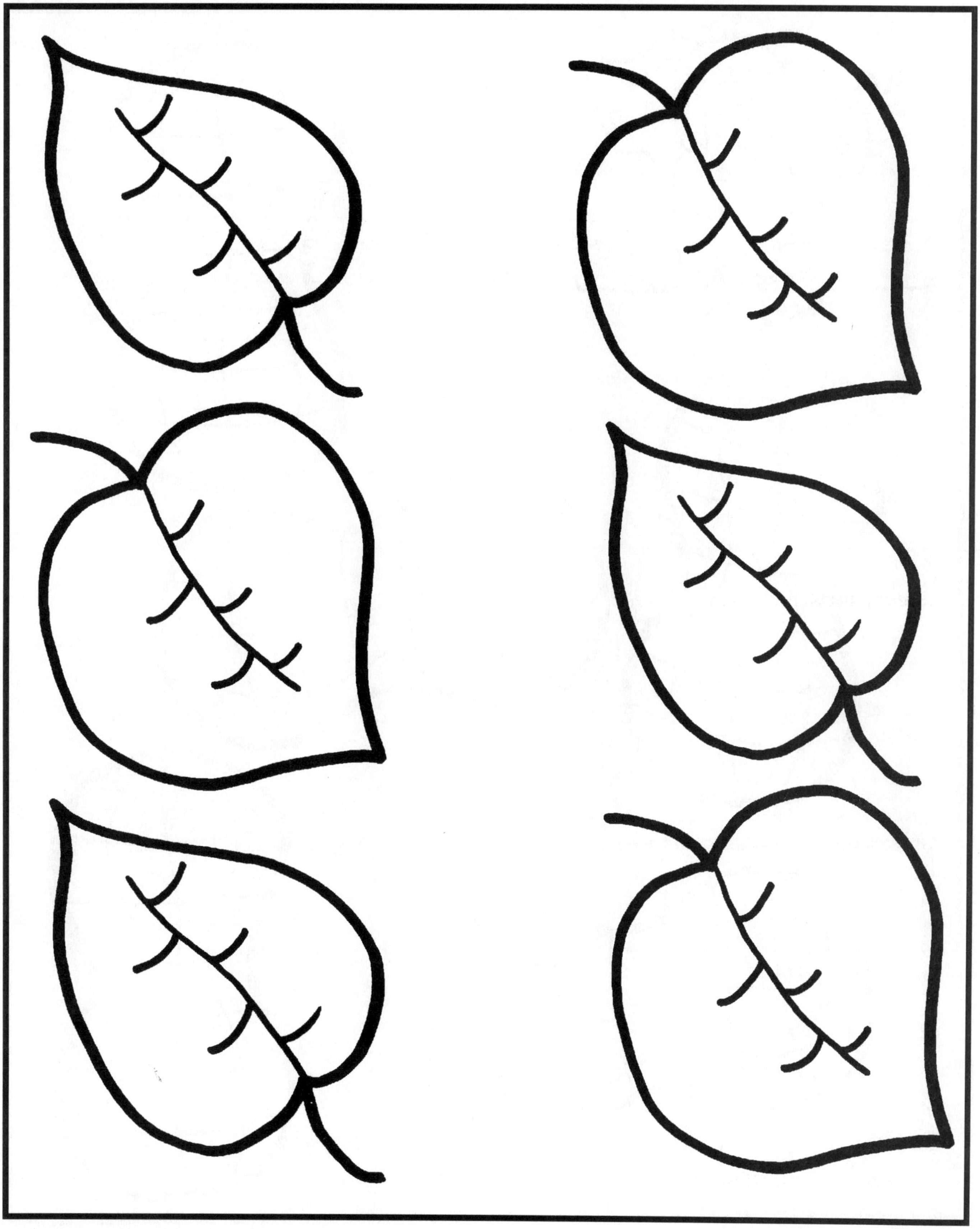

Name ______________________________ Skill: Cutting peanuts

Color the peanuts brown.

✂ Cut out the peanuts.

Name ______________________________ Skill: Cutting raindrops

Color the raindrops blue.

✂ Cut out the rain drops.

©1995 Kelley Wingate Publications, Inc.

Name ______________________________ Skill: Cutting fish

Color each fish a different color.

✂ Cut out the fish.

Name ______________________________ Skill: Cutting baseballs

Color each baseball a different color.

✂ Cut out all of the baseballs.

Name ______________________________ Skill: Completing objects

Finish the second shape by making it look like the first one.

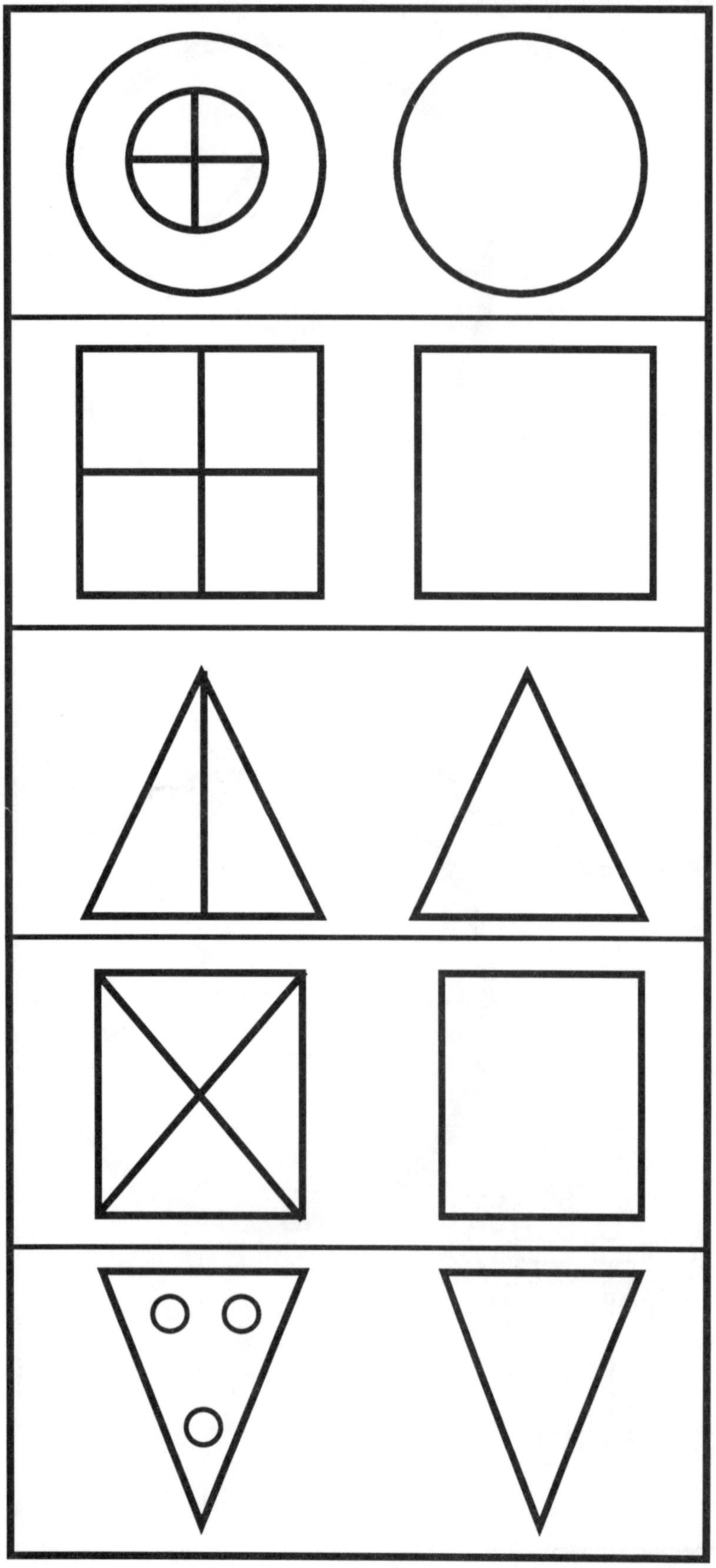

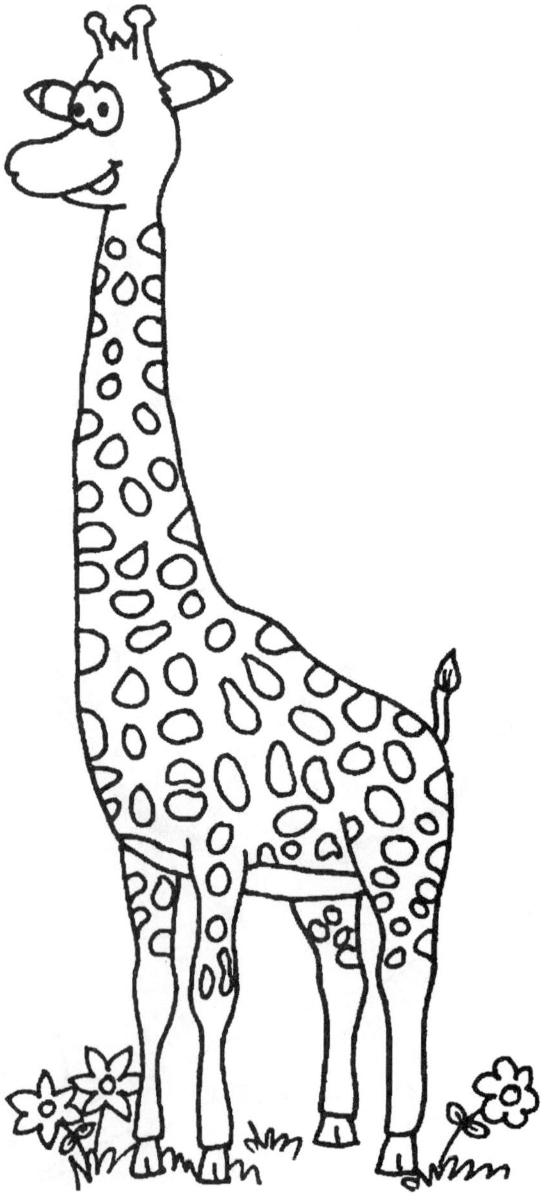

Name ______________________________ Skill: Completing objects

Finish the second shape by making it look like the first one.

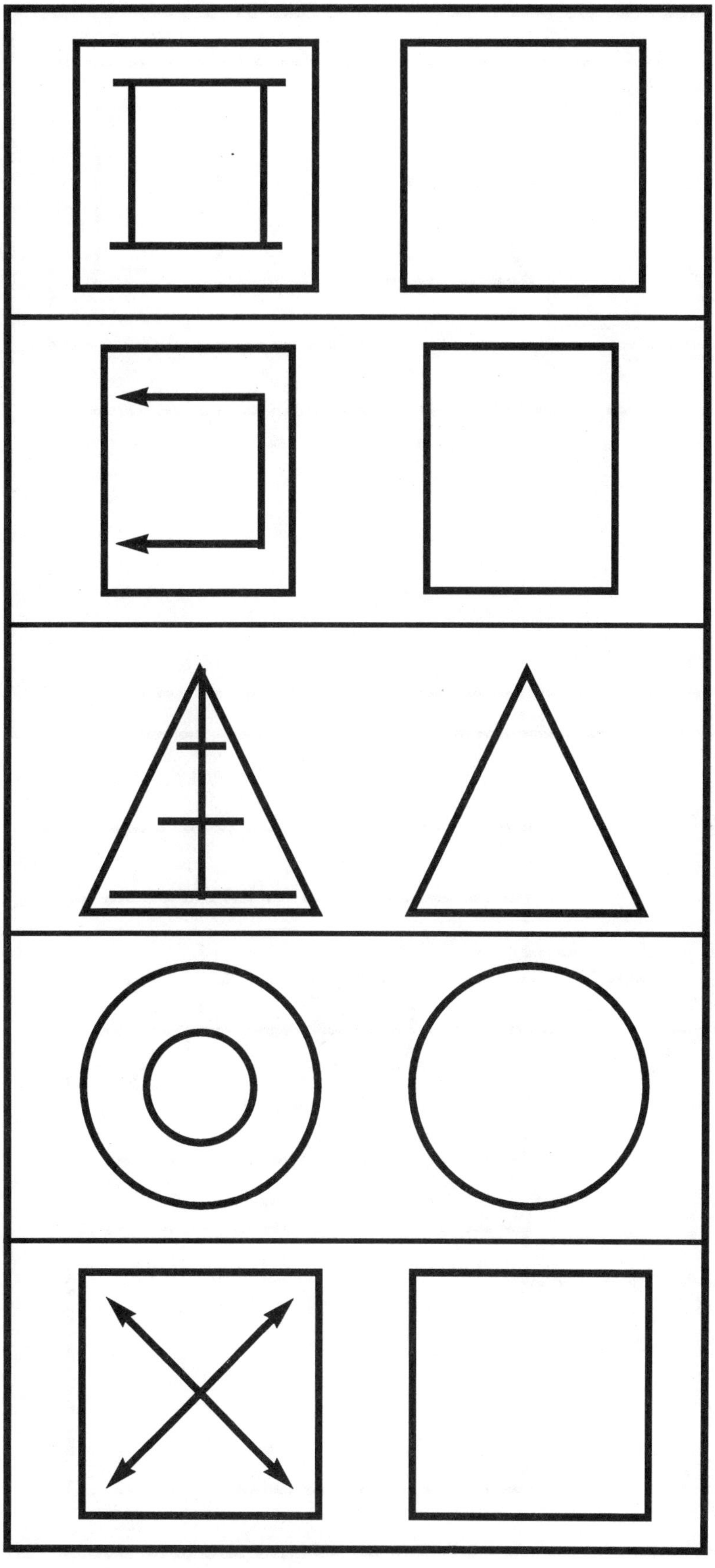

©1995 Kelley Wingate Publications, Inc.

Name ______________________________ Skill: Cutting straight lines

Trace over the dotted lines to complete the shapes.
Make the bottom shape look like the top shape.

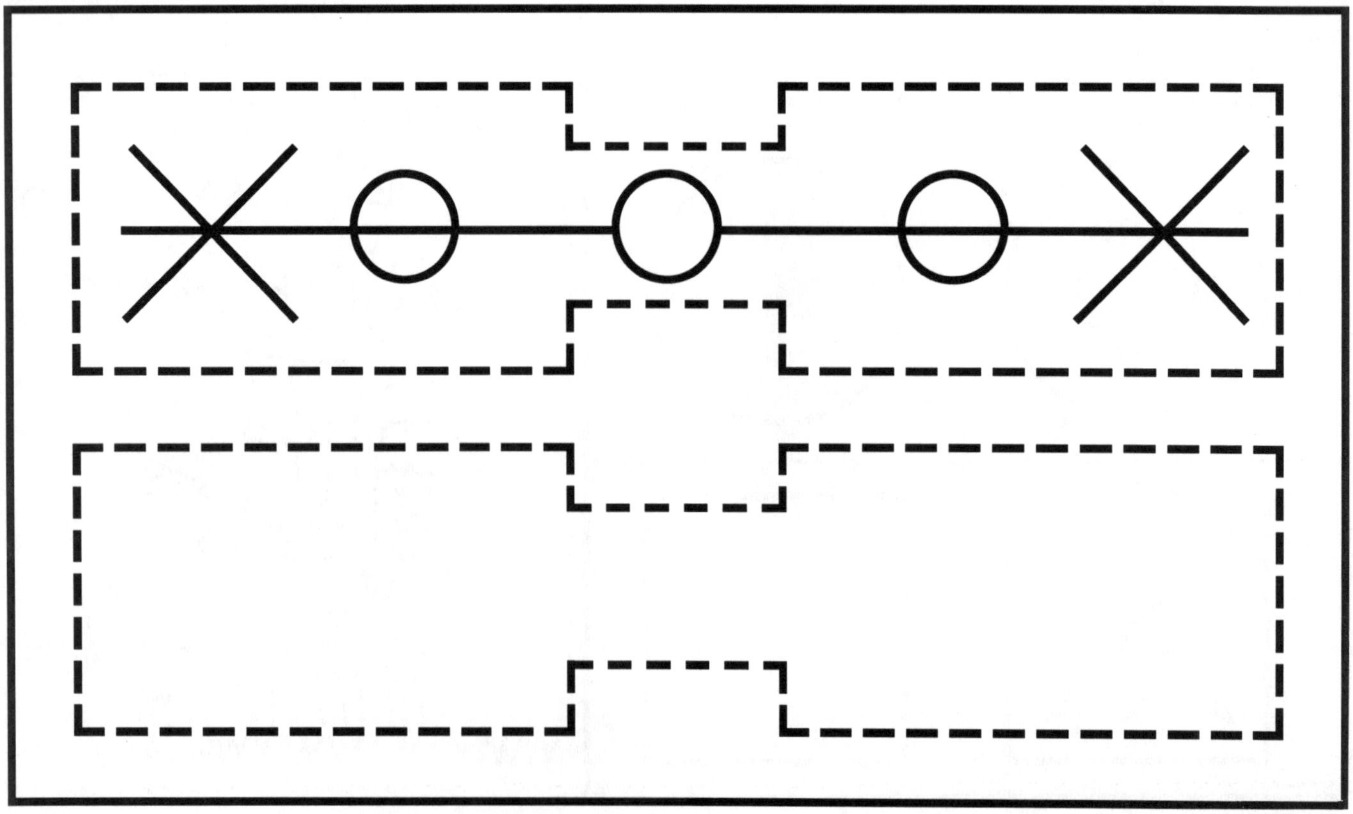

©1995 Kelley Wingate Publications, Inc.

Name ______________________________ Skill: Cutting straight lines

Trace over the dotted lines to complete the shapes.
Make the second shape look like the first shape.

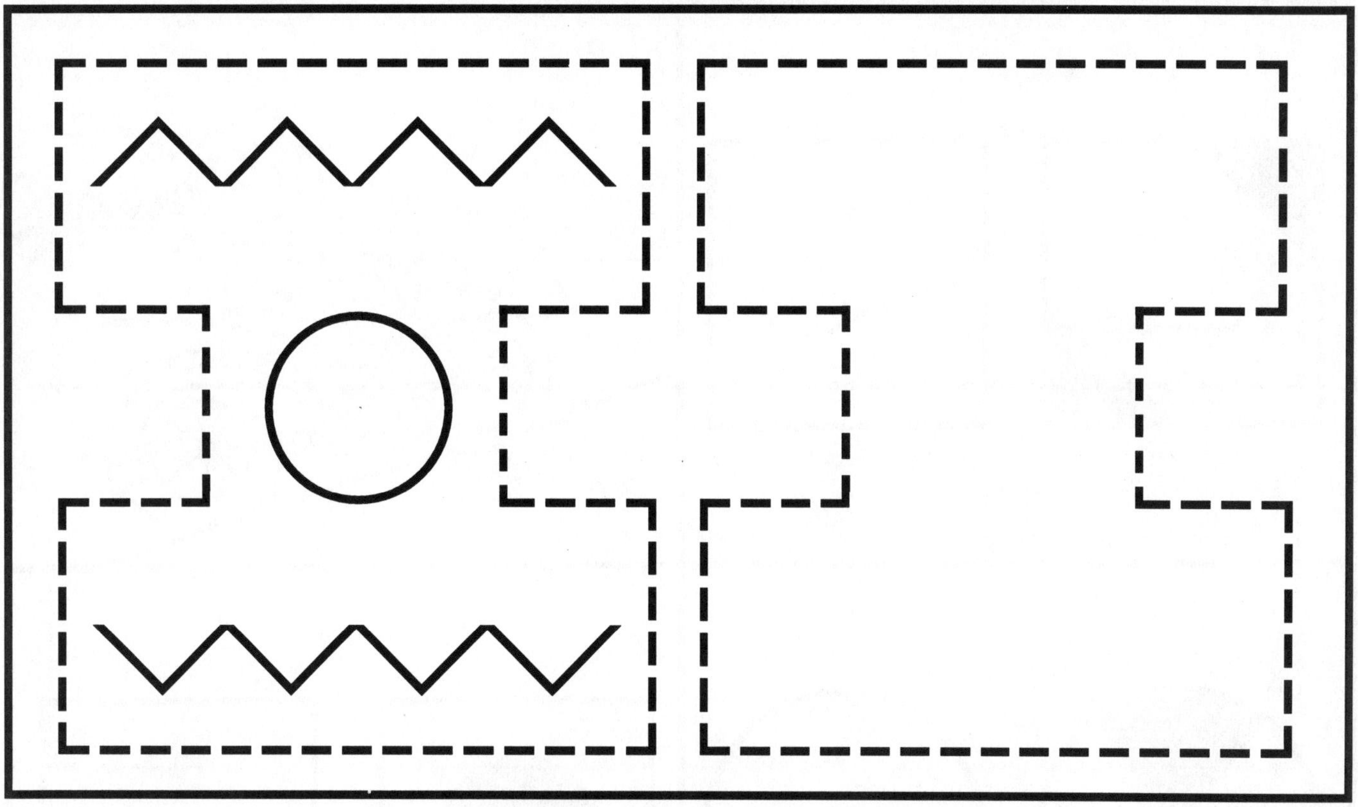

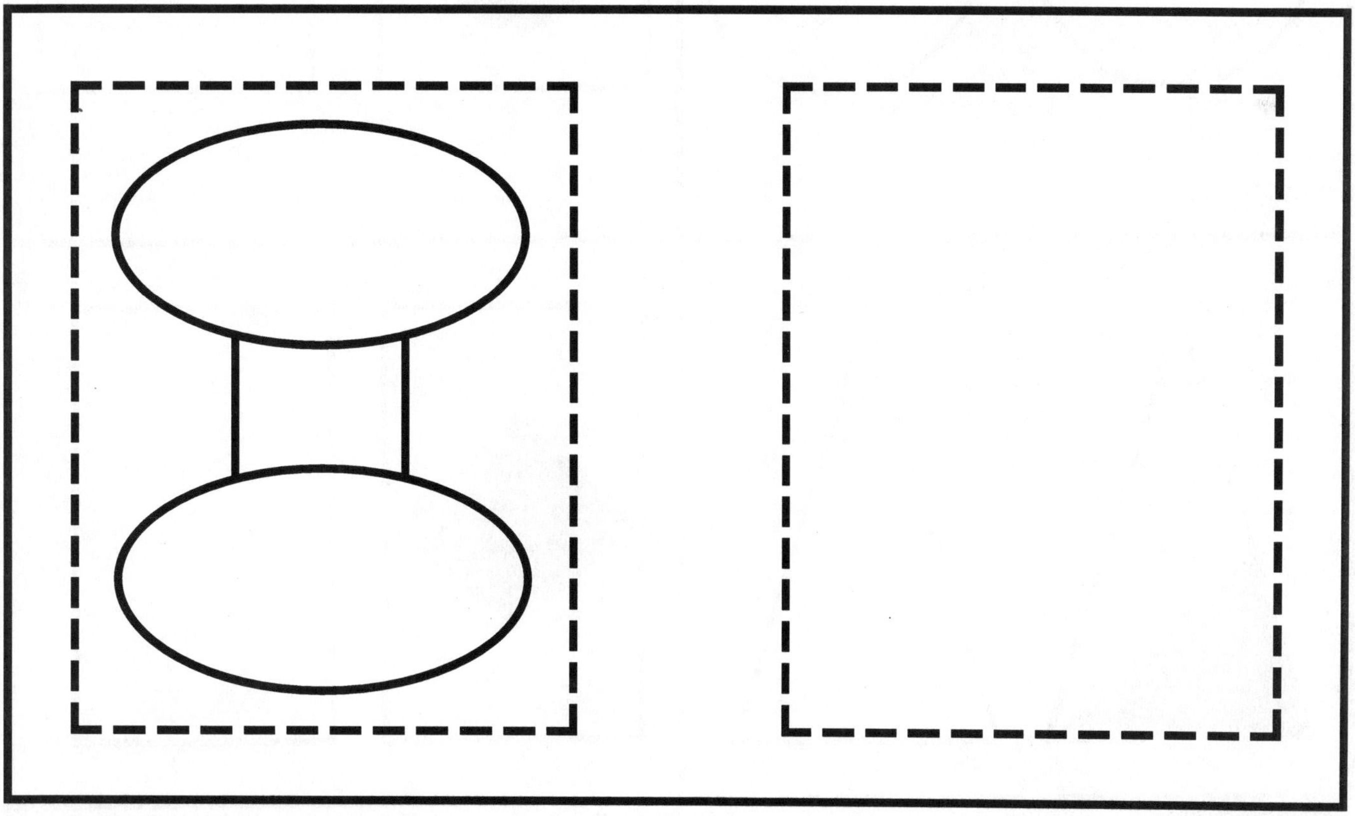

Name ______________________________ Skill: Completing objects

In each box color the second shape to make it look like the first shape.

Name ______________________________ Skill: Compleing objects

In each box color the second shape to make it look like the first shape.

©1995 Kelley Wingate Publications, Inc.

Name ______________________________ Skill: Completing a snowman

Make the right half of the snowman look like the left half of the snowman. Color the completed picture.

Name ______________________________ Skill: Completing a vase

Make the left half of the vase look like the right half of the vase. Color the completed picture.

Name ______________________ Skill: Completing a heart

Make the right half of the heart look like the left half of the heart. Color the completed picture.

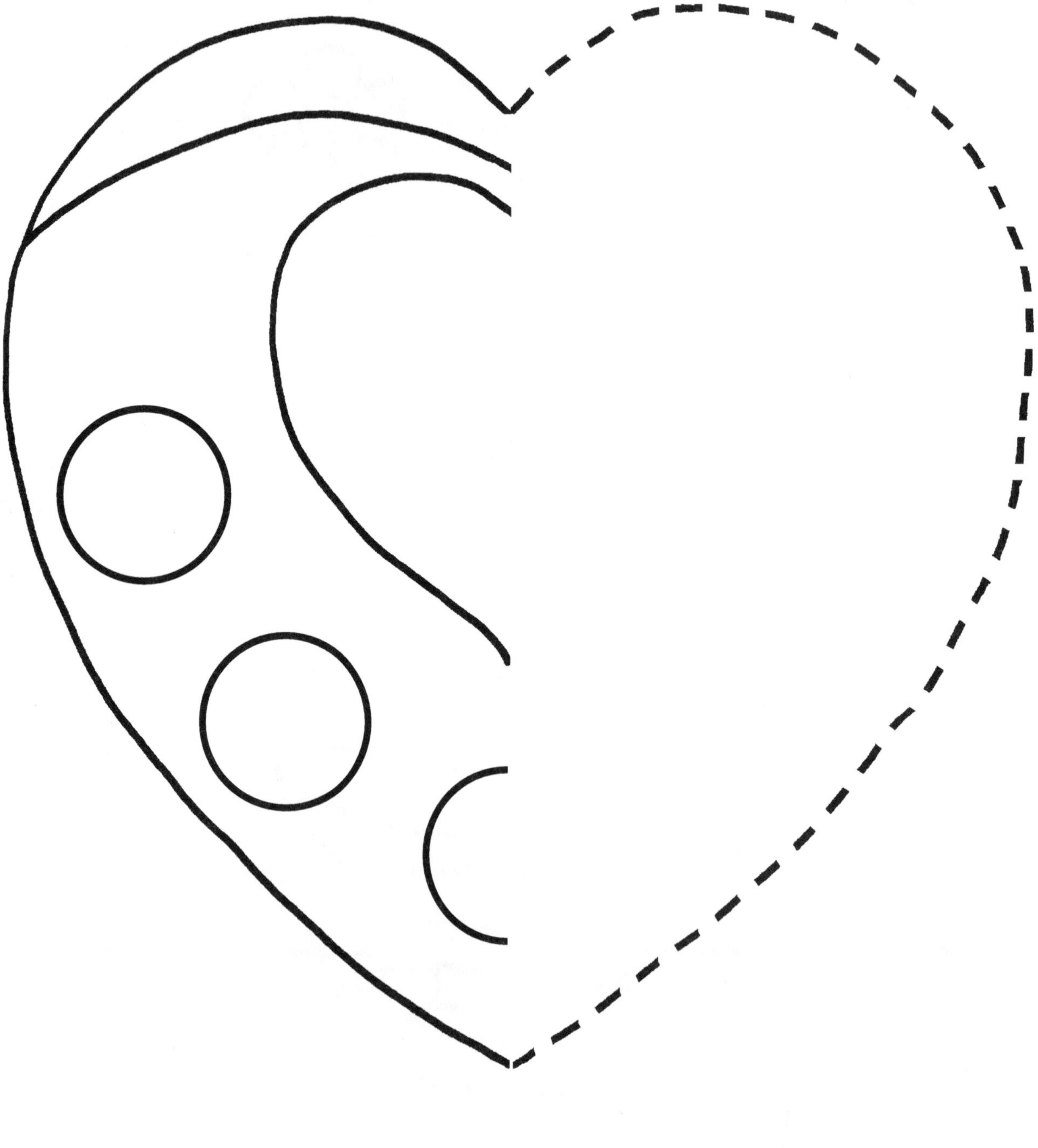

Name ______________________________ Skill: Completing a fish

Follow the example given below to draw your own fish.
Color the completed fish.

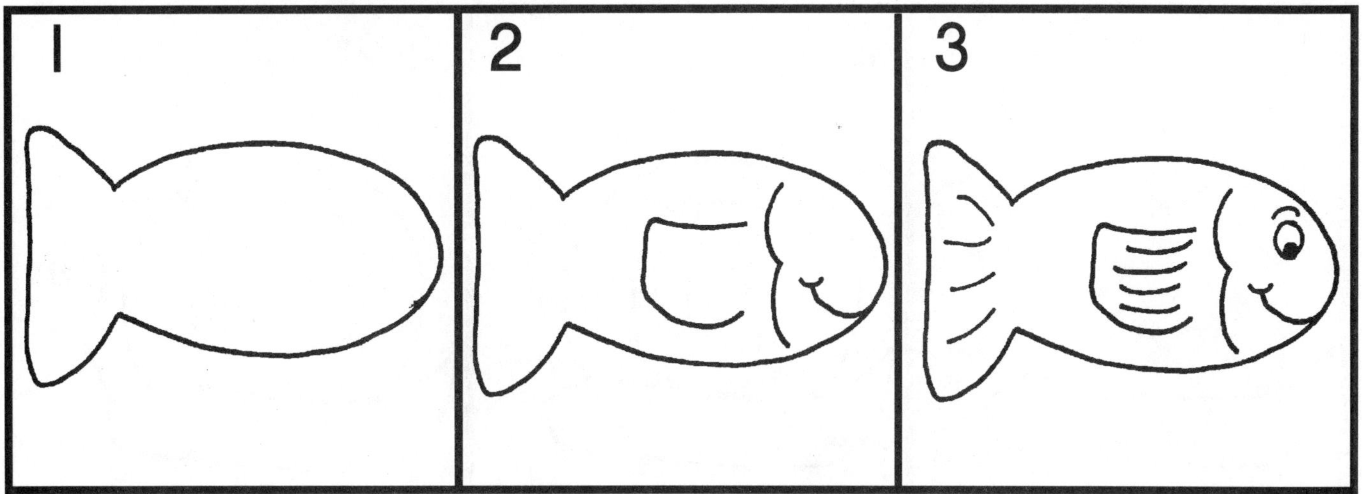

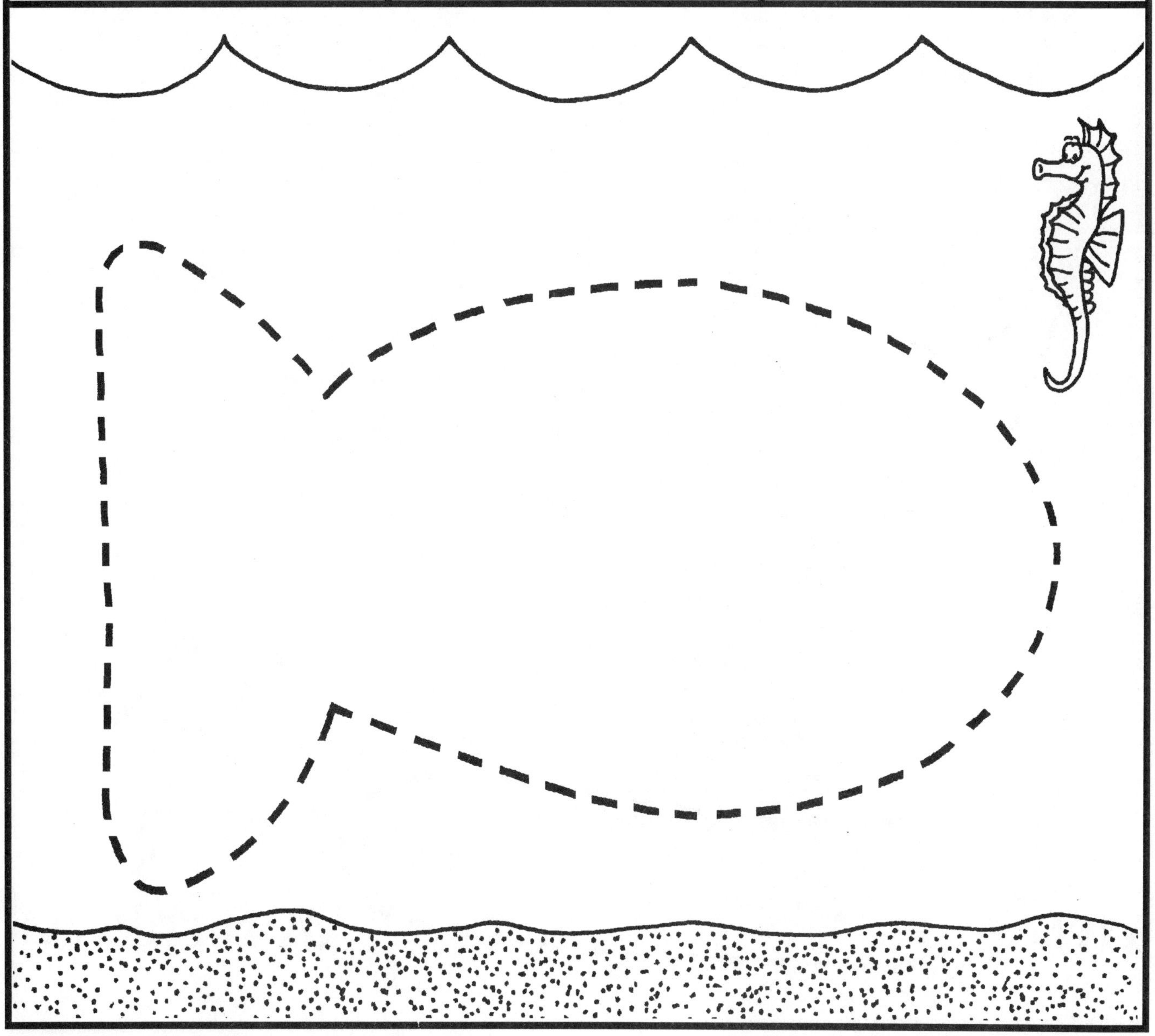

Name ______________________________ Skill: Completing a snail

Follow the example given below to draw a smiling snail. Color the completed snail.

1

2

3

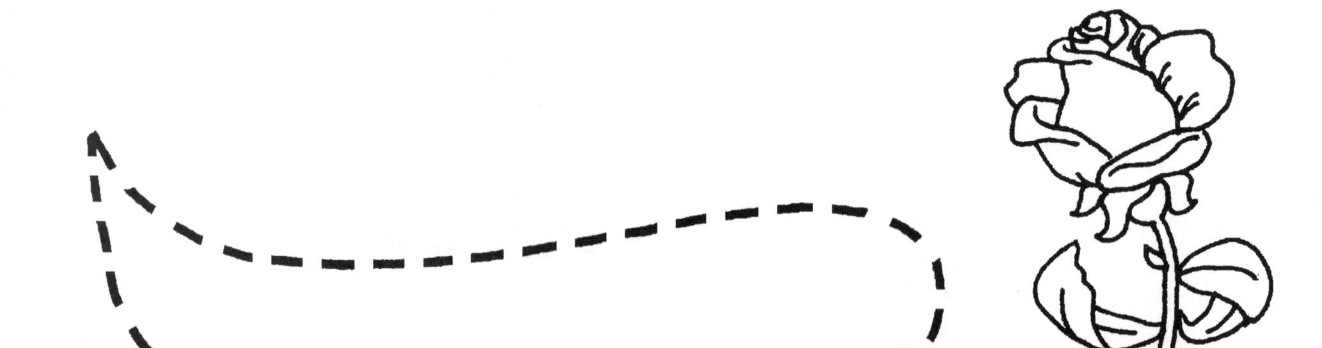

©1995 Kelley Wingate Publications, Inc.

Name ____ Skill: Completing a butterfly

Follow the example given below to draw your own happy butterfly. Color the completed butterfly.

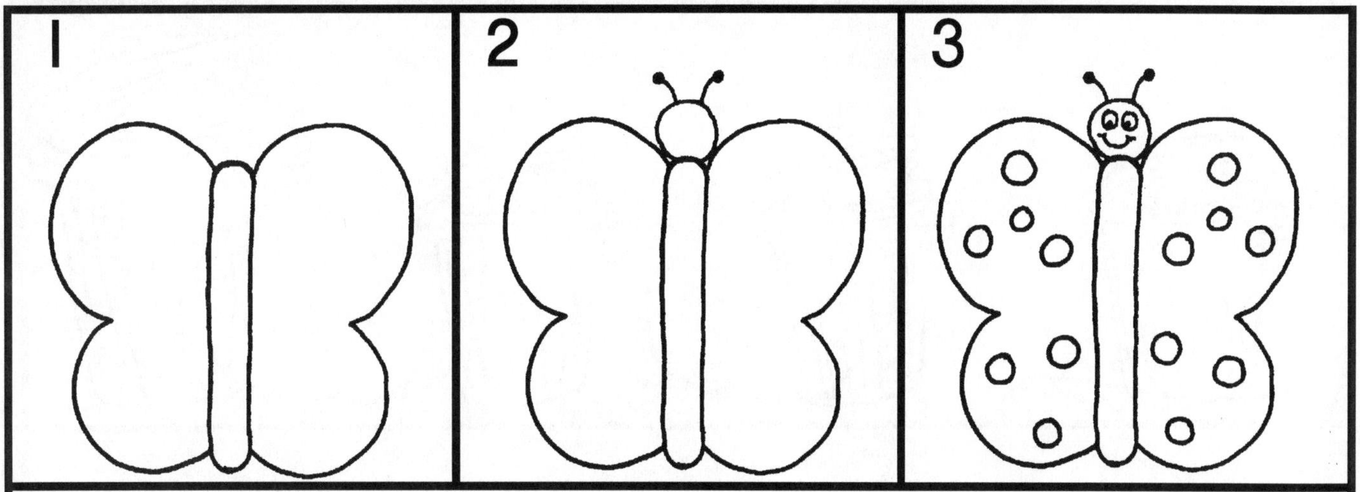

©1995 Kelley Wingate Publications, Inc.

Name ______________________________ Skill: Comparing size

In each row circle and color the largest object.

©1995 Kelley Wingate Publications, Inc.

Name ____________________ Skill: Comparing size

Color all of the big frogs green.

Draw a circle around the small frogs.

Name ______________________________ Skill: Comparing size

Color all of the small apples red.
Color all of the large apples green.

Name ______________________________ Skill: Comparing size

In each box circle and color the smallest object.

©1995 Kelley Wingate Publications, Inc.

Name ______________________________ Skill: Comparing size

In each box circle and color the largest object.

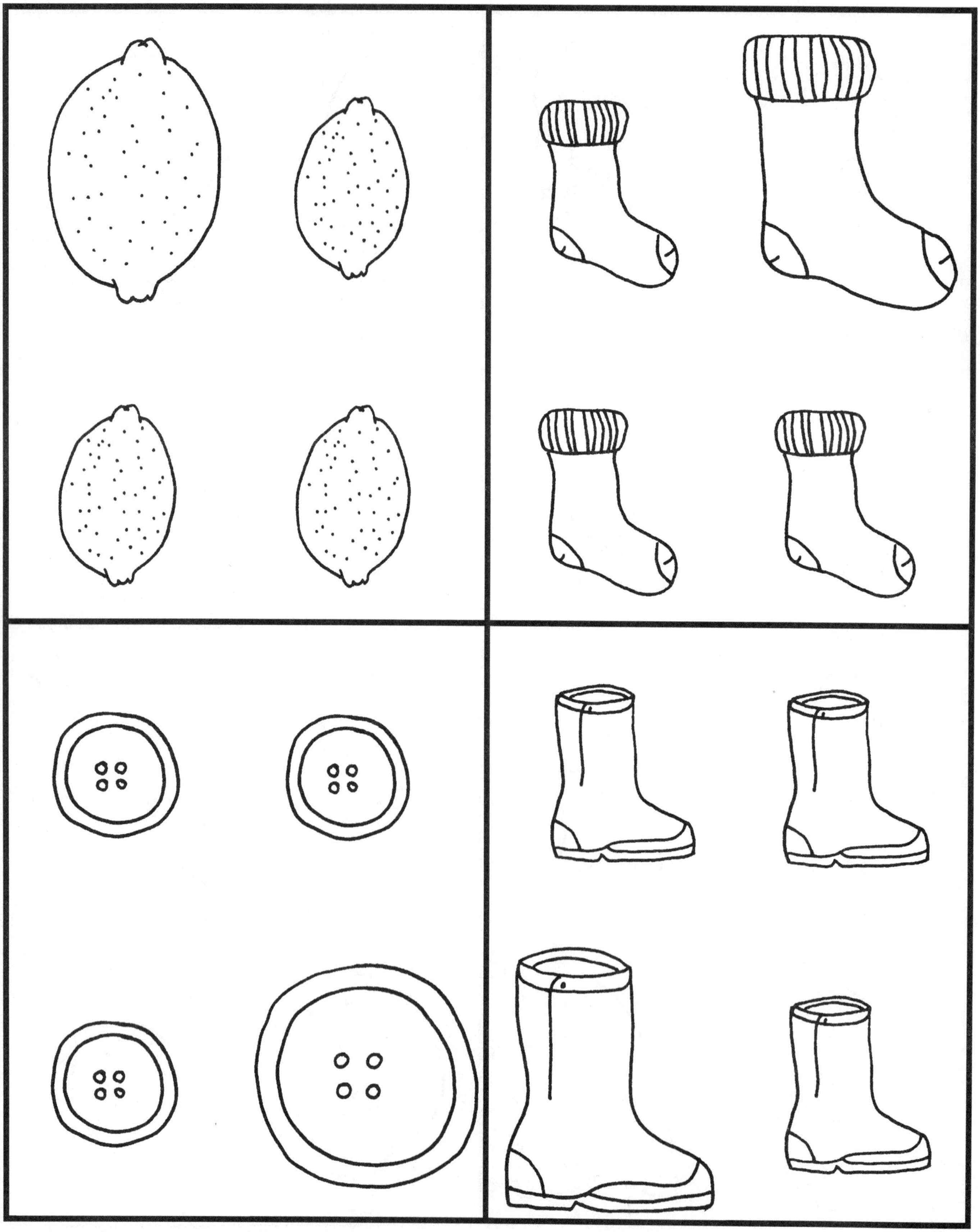

©1995 Kelley Wingate Publications, Inc.

Name ______________________________ Skill: Comparing length

In each box circle and color the shorter object.

©1995 Kelley Wingate Publications, Inc.

Name ______________________________ Skill: Comparing length

Color the long bats orange. Color the short bats blue.

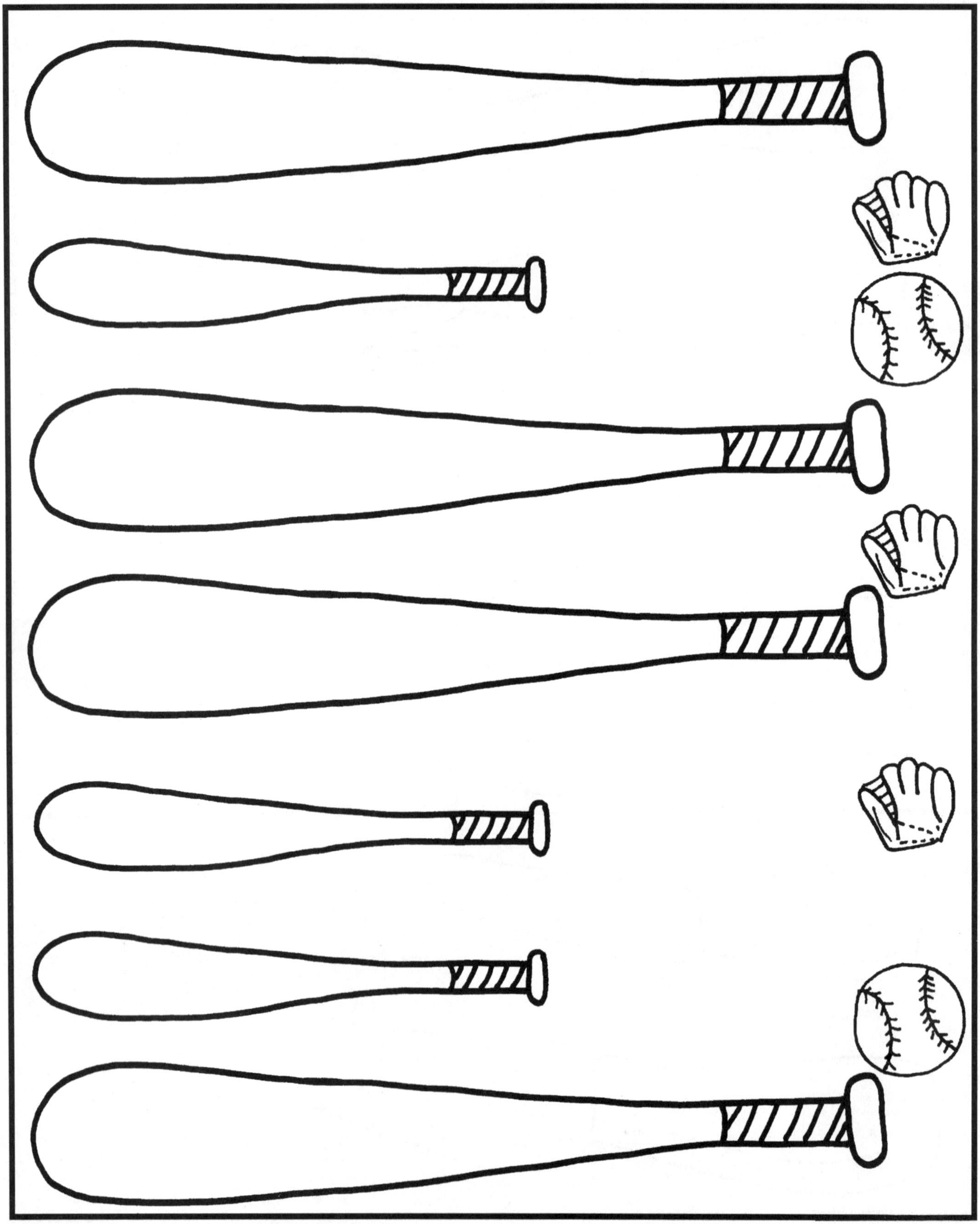

©1995 Kelley Wingate Publications, Inc.

Name ____________________ Skill: Comparing length

Color the long paint brushes red.
Color the short paint brushes yellow.

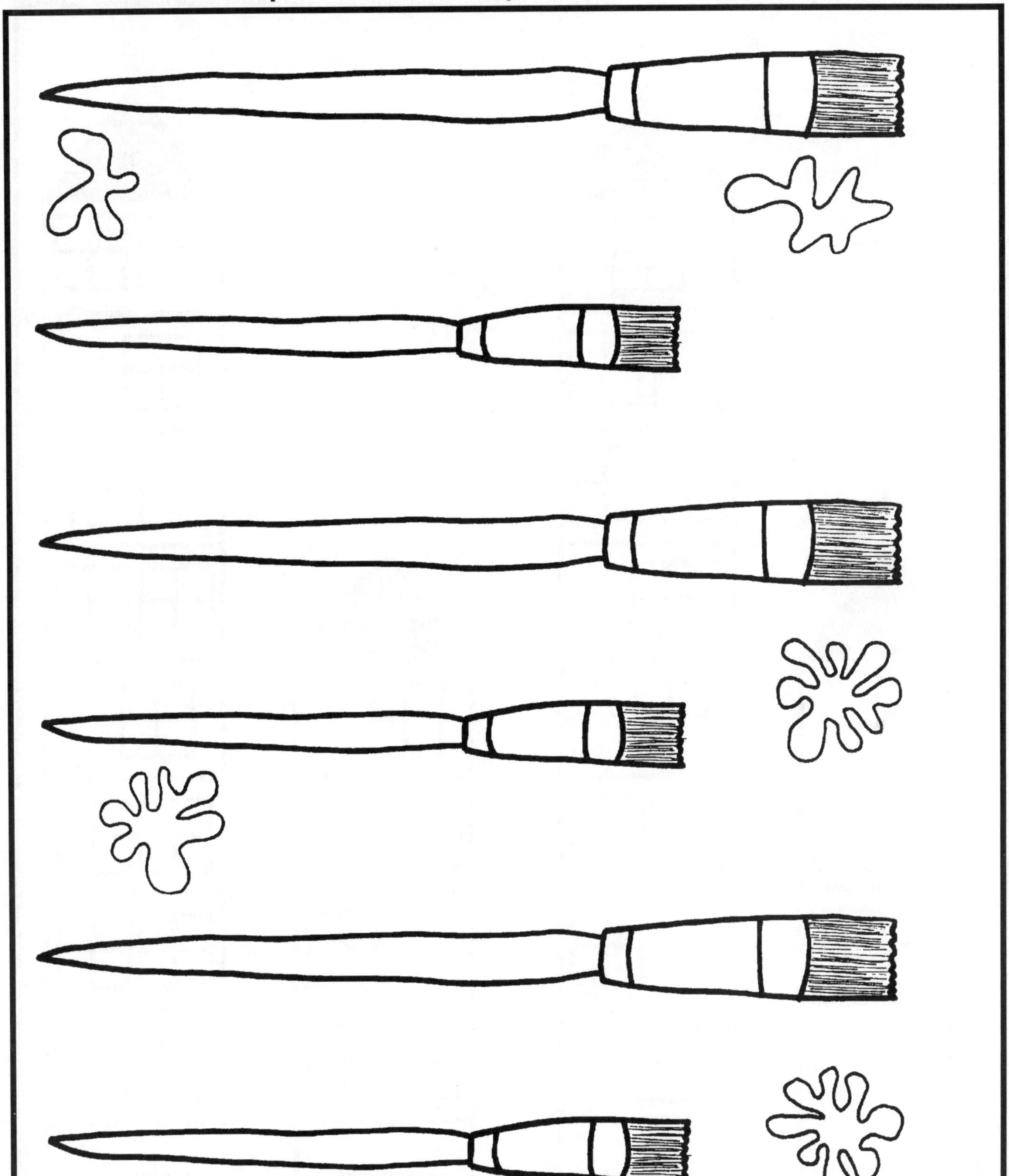

©1995 Kelley Wingate Publications, Inc.

Name ____________________ Skill: Comparing length

Color the tall buildings purple. Color the short buildings red.

Name ___________________________________

Skill: Recognizing Likeness and differences

In each box circle and color the two objects that are the same.

©1995 Kelley Wingate Publications, Inc.

Name ___________________________________

Skill: Recognizing Likeness and differences

Draw a line to match the ice cream cones that are the same.

Name ______________________________

Skill: Recognizing Likeness and differences

Color the balls that are the same as the ball in the box.

Name ______________________________

Skill: Recognizing Likeness and differences

Color all of the hats that are the same as the hat on the top of the hat rack.

Name ____________________________________

In each box circle the object that is different than the others and color the objects that are the same.

Name ______________________________

Skill: Recognizing likeness and differences

Circle and color the object that is different in each row.

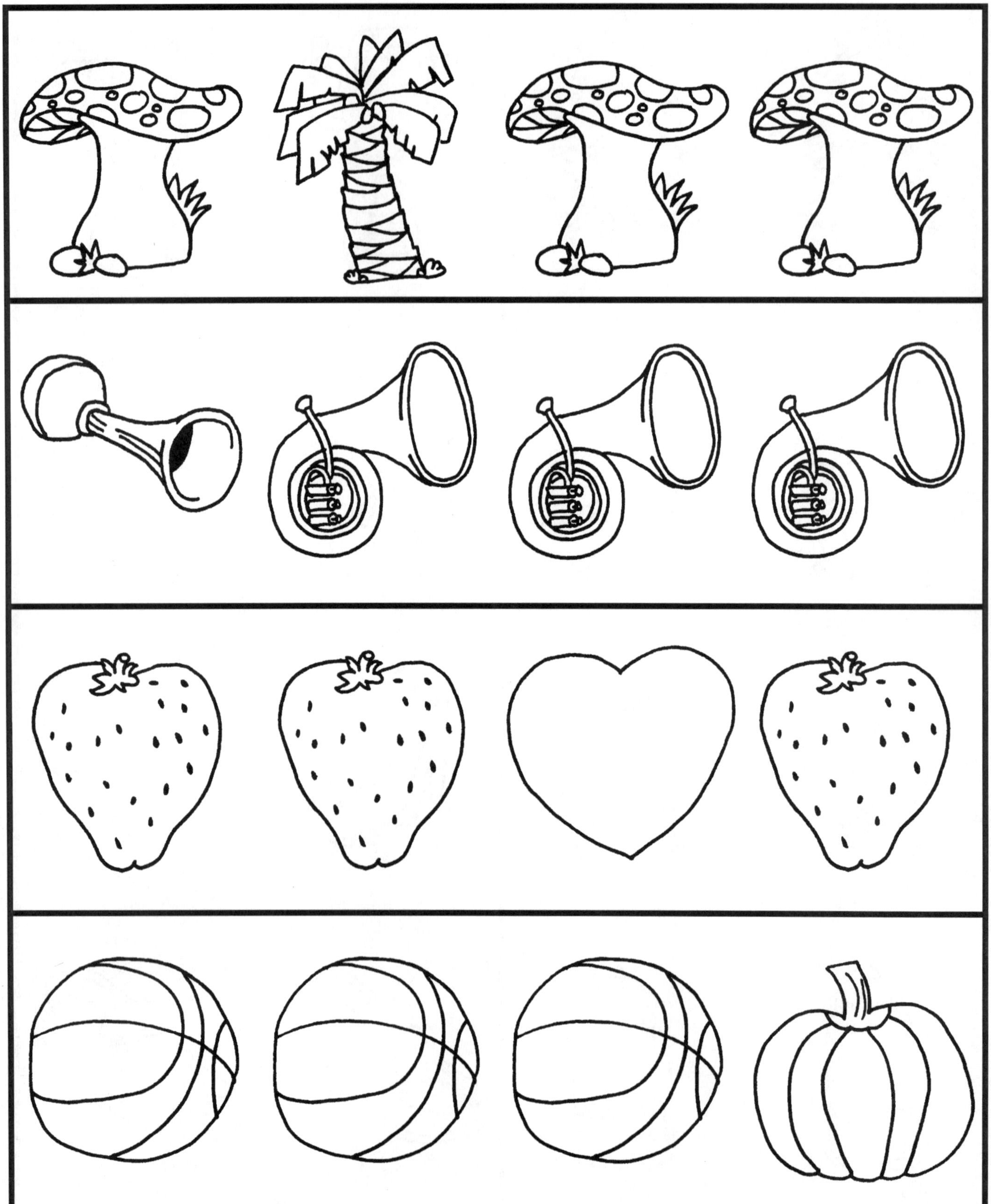

Name ______________________________________

Skill: Recognizing likeness and differences

Color the eggs that are <u>different</u> than the one that the bunny is holding.

Name ______________________________

Skill: Recognizing likeness and differences

Color the squares that are different than the top square.

©1995 Kelley Wingate Publications, Inc.

Name ________________________________

Skill: Recognizing likeness and differences

In each row color the shape that is different.

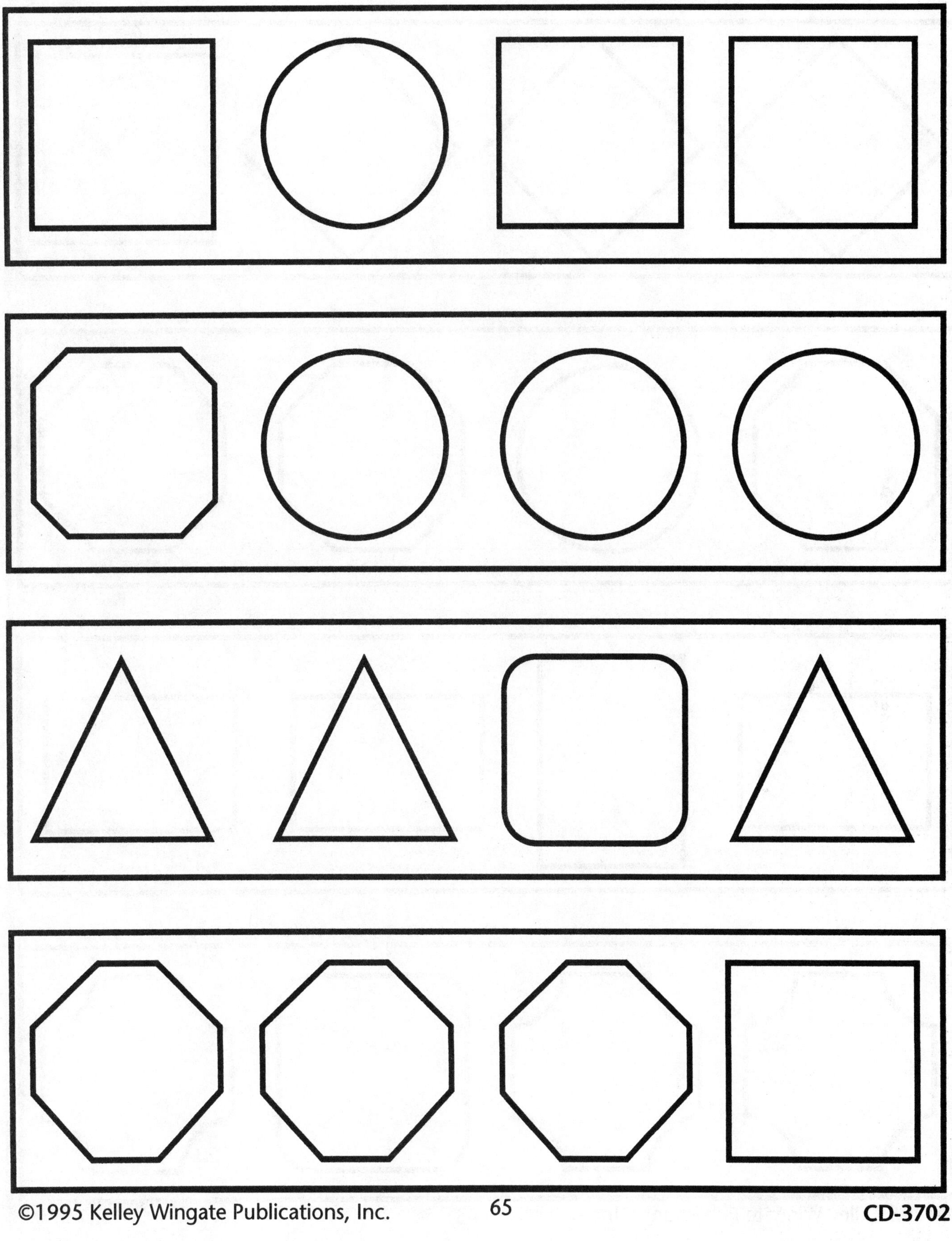

Name____________________

Skill: Recognizing likeness and differences

In each row color the shape that is different.

©1995 Kelley Wingate Publications, Inc.

Name ______________________________

Skill: Recognizing likeness and differences

In each box color the two shapes that are the same.

Name ______________________________________

Skill: Recognizing likeness and differences

In each box circle and color the two shapes that are the same.

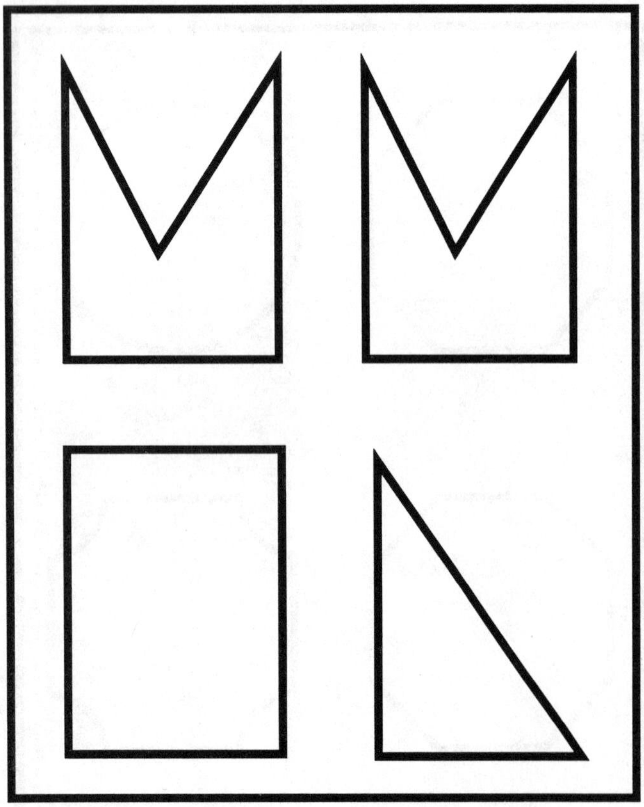

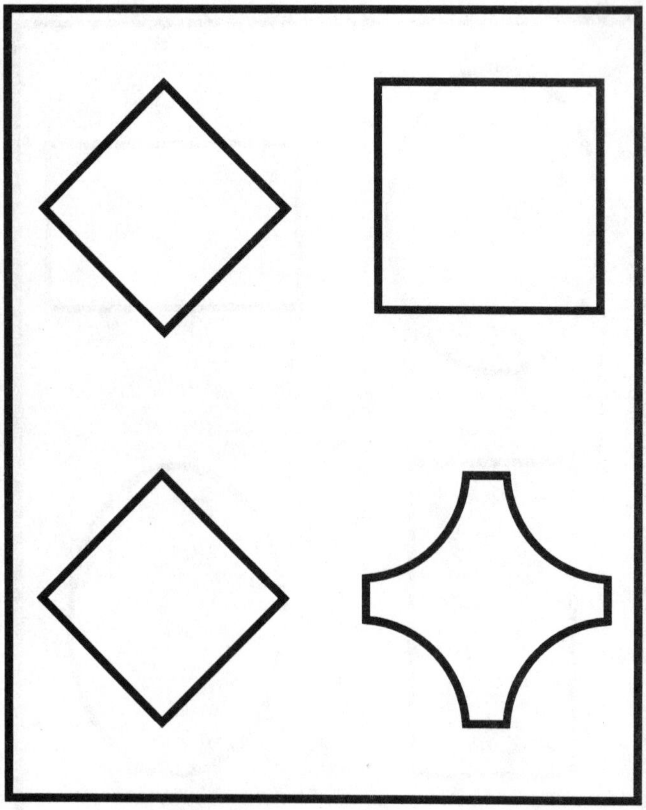

Name ______________________________

Skill: Identifying rectangles and ovals

Color the ovals orange.
Color the rectangles green.

©1995 Kelley Wingate Publications, Inc.

Name ________________________________

Skill: Identifying circles and squares

Color the squares brown. Color the circles blue.

©1995 Kelley Wingate Publications, Inc.

Name ______________________________

Skill: Identifying diamonds and triangles

Color the triangles red. Color the diamonds yellow.

Name ______________________________ Skill: Identifying circles

Find and color 6 circles.

Name____________________ Skill: Identifying circles

Find and color 4 circles hidden in the clocks.

©1995 Kelley Wingate Publications, Inc.

Name ____________________ Skill: Identifying squares

Find and color 8 squares.

Name ______________________________ Skill: Identifying squares

Find and color the squares.

Name ____ Skill: Identifying rectangles

Can you find and color 5 rectangles hidden in this birthday cake?

Name ____________________________________ Skill: Identifying triangles

Color the triangles red. Color all of the other shapes green.

Name ______________________________ Skill: Identifying circles

Color the circles purple. Color all of the other shapes pink.

©1995 Kelley Wingate Publications, Inc.

Name ______________________________ Skill: Identifying squares

Color the squares brown. Color all of the other shapes red.

Name ______________________________ Skill: Identifying rectangles

Find and color the rectangles orange. Color all of the other shapes blue.

Name ______________________________ Skill: Tracing shapes

Trace over the dotted lines to complete the shapes.

square

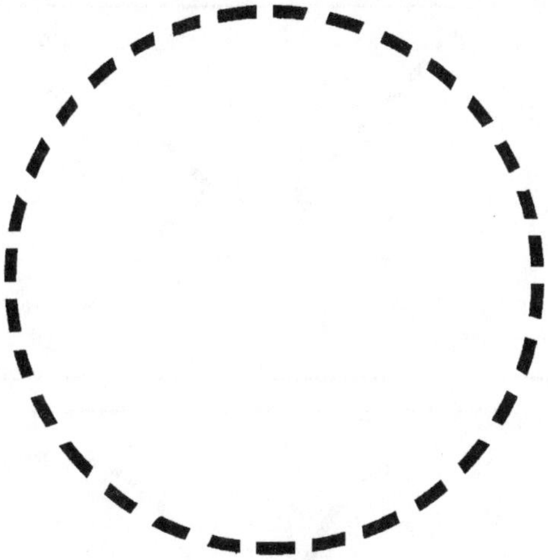

circle

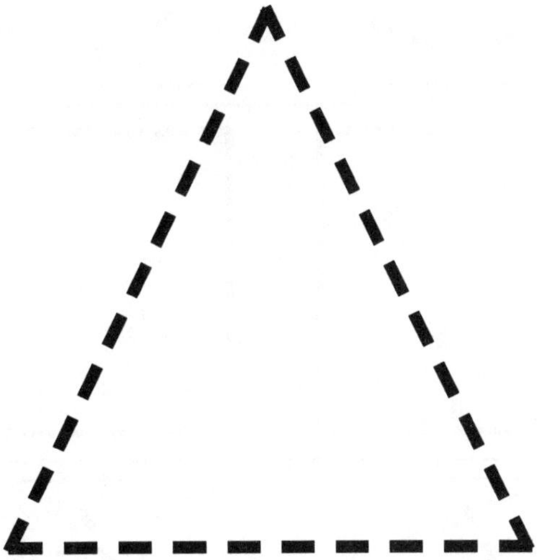

triangle

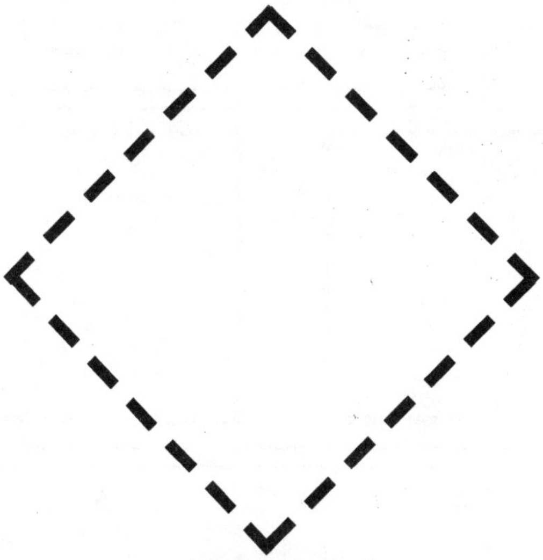

diamond

rectangle

oval

©1995 Kelley Wingate Publications, Inc.

Name ____________________ Skill: Reviewing shapes

Trace over the dotted lines to practice drawing each shape.

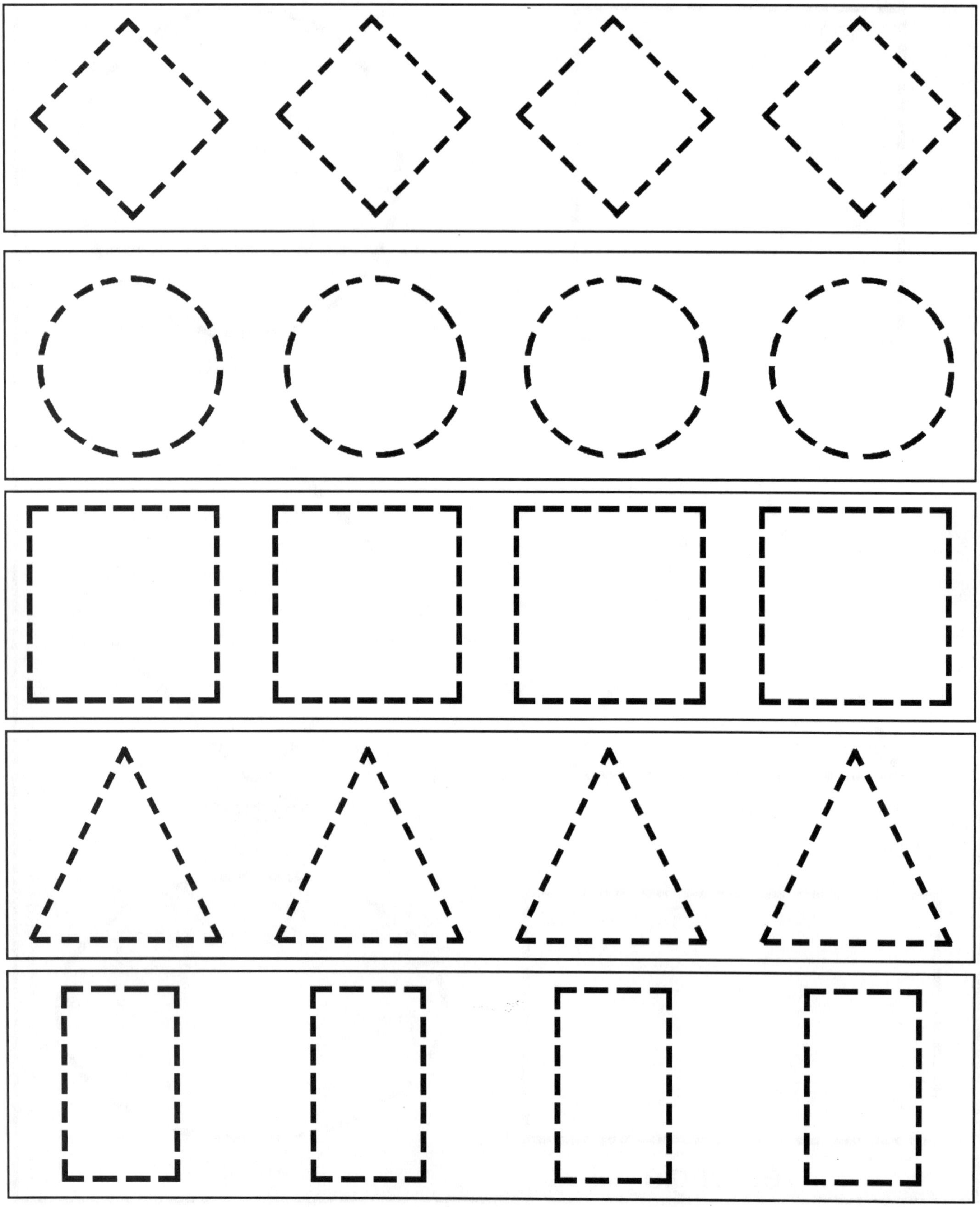

©1995 Kelley Wingate Publications, Inc.

Name ____________________________________ Skill: Reviewing shapes

Draw a line to match the shapes that are the same. Color the matching shapes the same color.

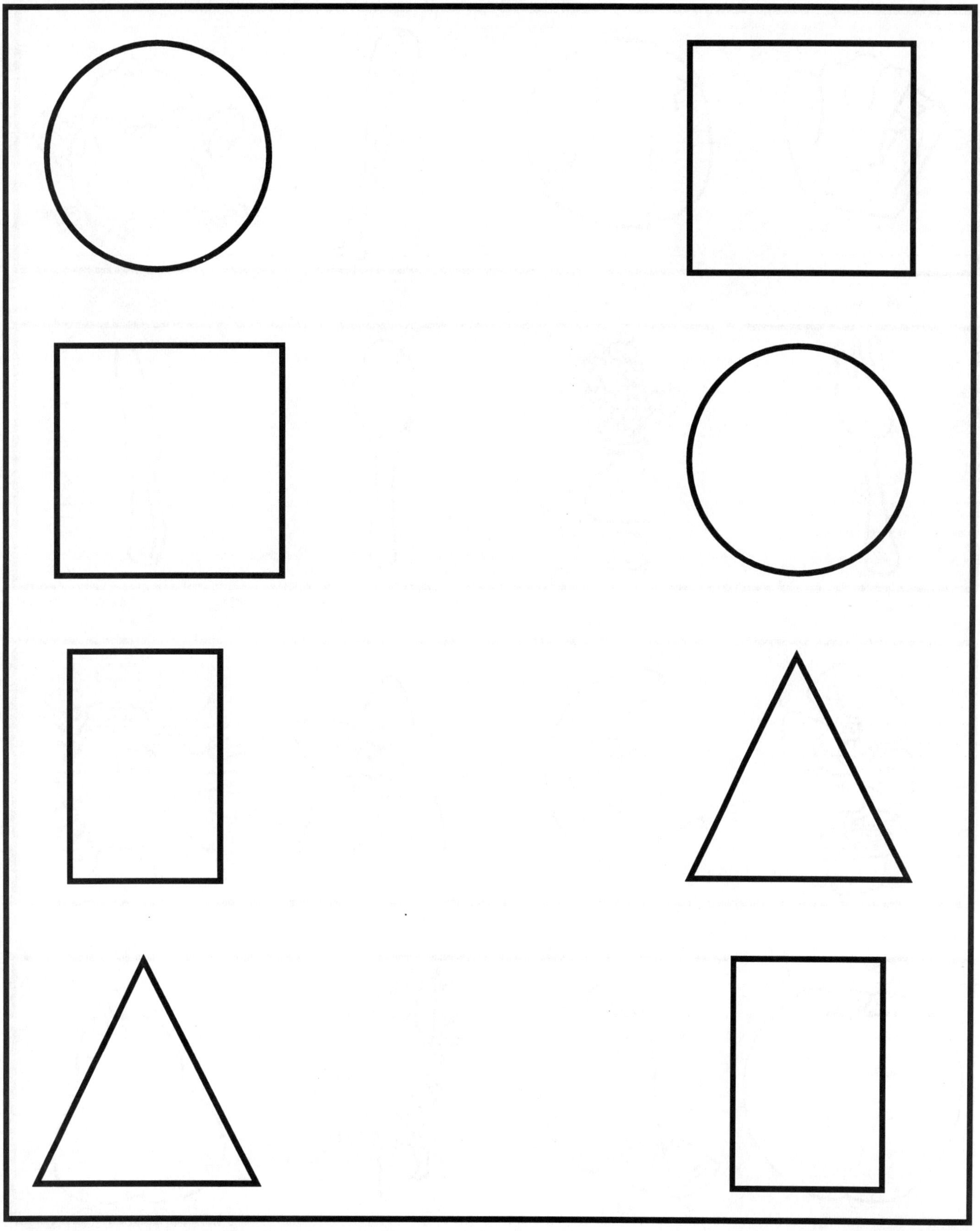

Name ______________________________ Skill: Identifying things that do not belong

In each row circle the object that does not belong.
Color the objects that go together.

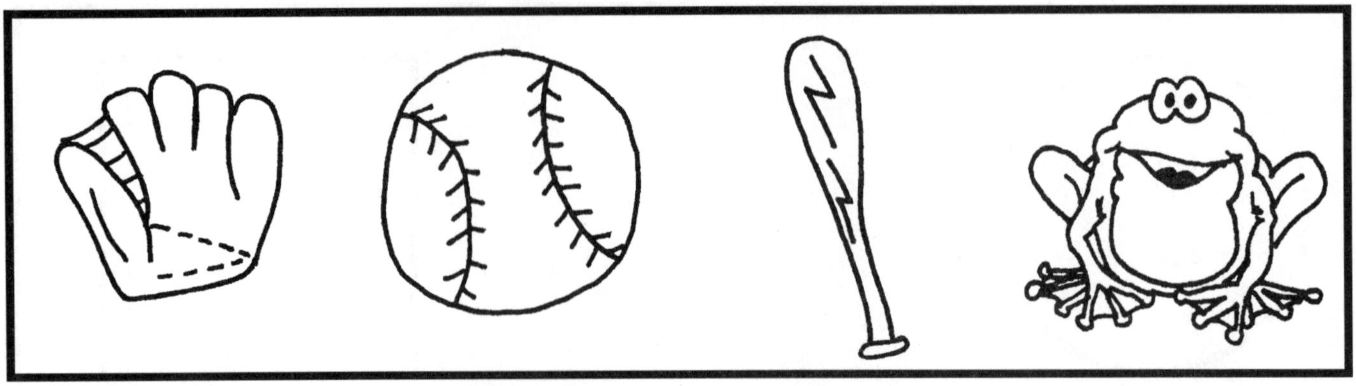

Name ____

Skill: Recognizing things that do not belong

In each row circle the picture that does not belong.

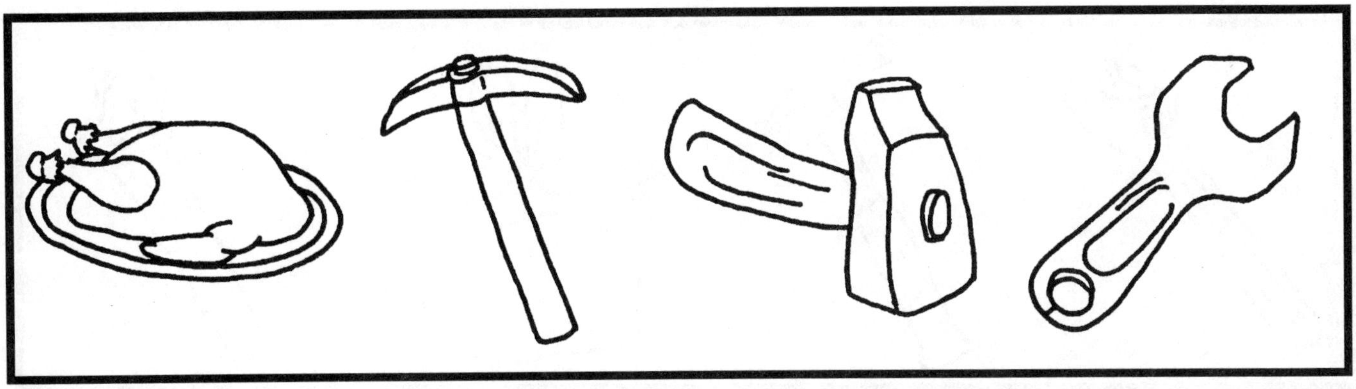

©1995 Kelley Wingate Publications, Inc.

Name ______________________________

Skill: Recognizing things that do not belong

In each row circle the picture that does not belong.

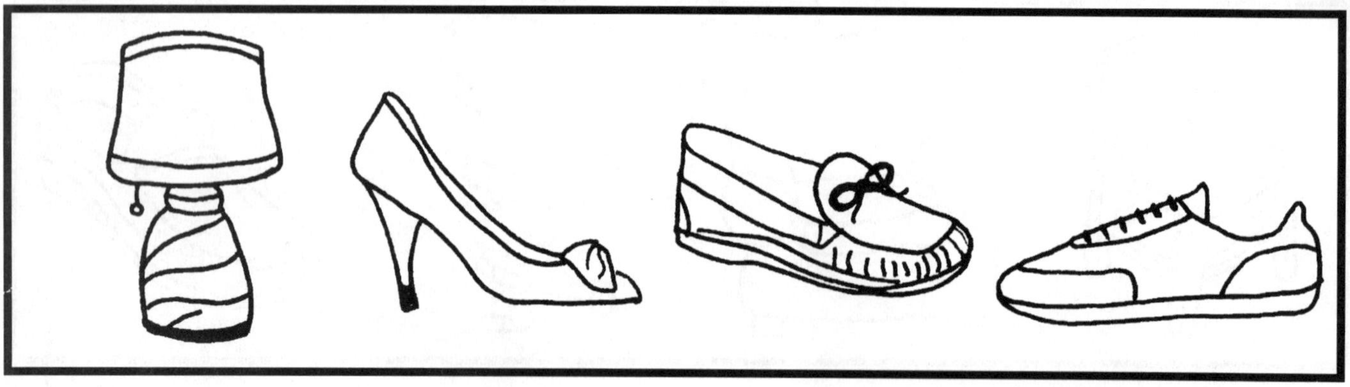

©1995 Kelley Wingate Publications, Inc.

Name ______________________________________ Skill: Recognizing things that do not belong

In each box put an "X" on the picture that does not belong.

©1995 Kelley Wingate Publications, Inc.

Name ______________________________

Skill: Identifying things that go together

In each row circle the three pictures that go together.

Name ______________________________

Skill: Recognizing things that go together

In each row circle the three pictures that go together.

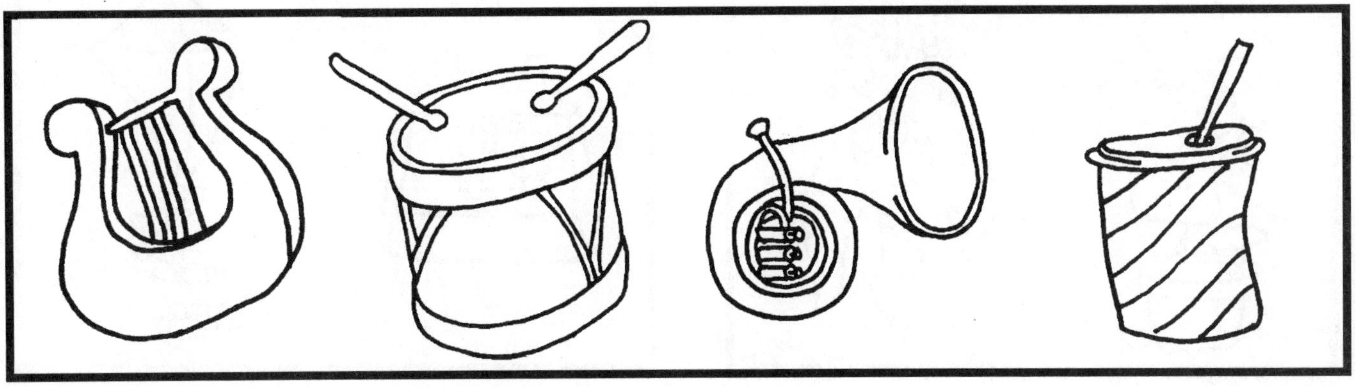

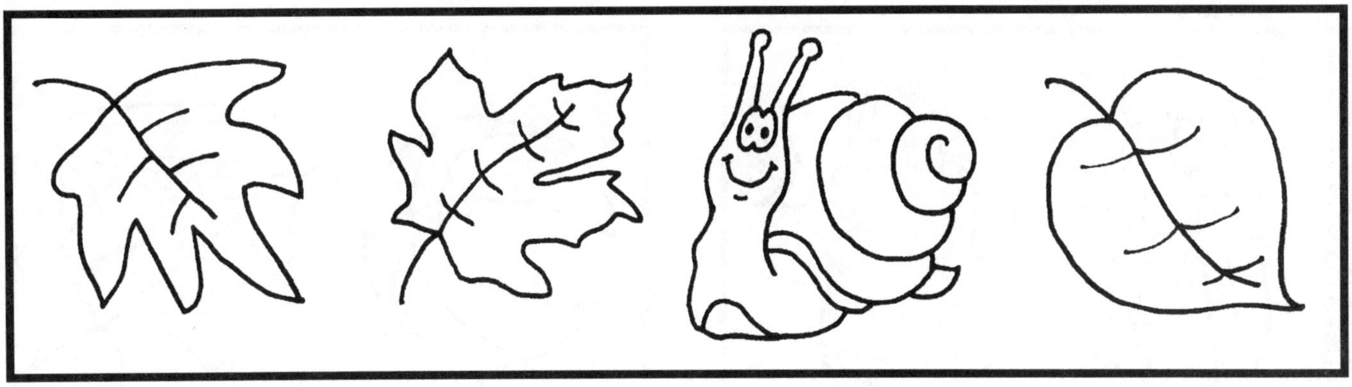

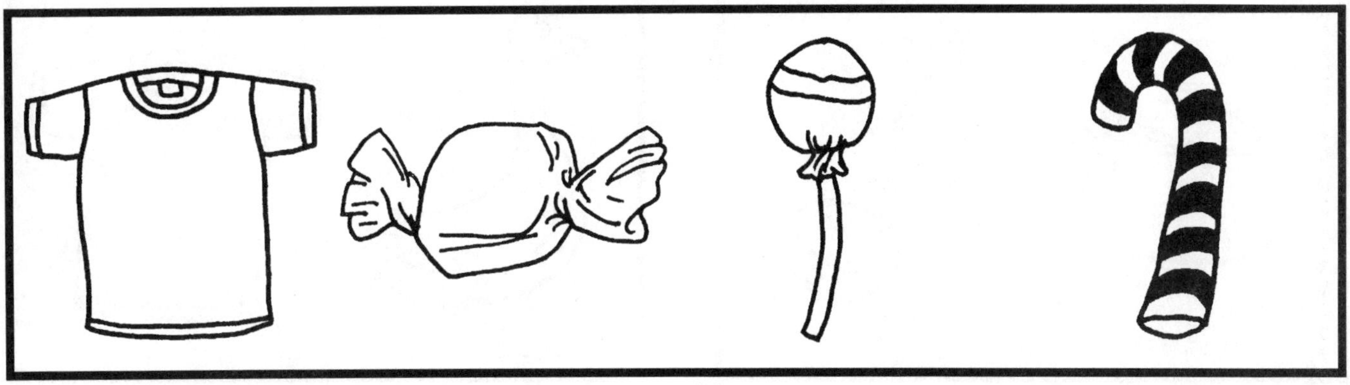

©1995 Kelley Wingate Publications, Inc.

Name ________________________________

Skill: Recognizing things that go together

In each box draw a line to match the two pictures that go together. Color each matching pair.

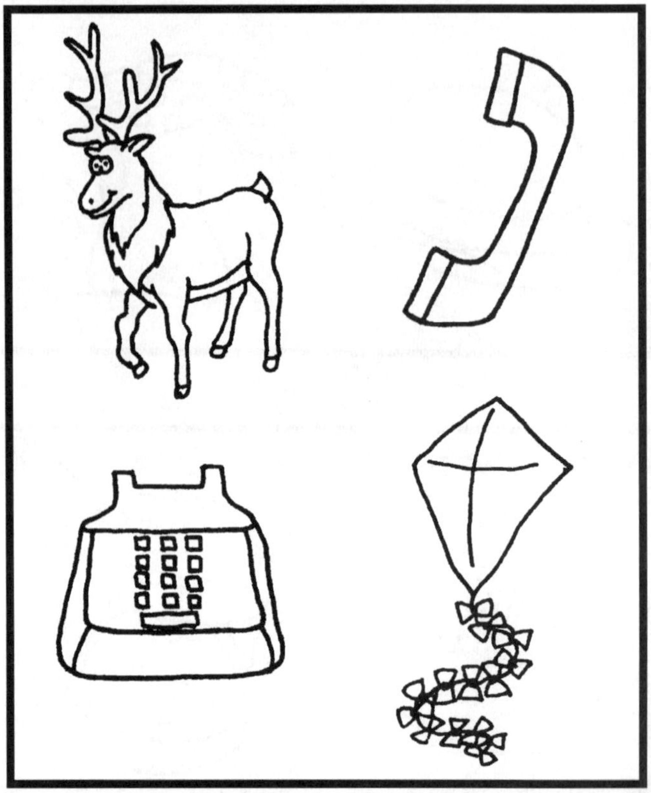

©1995 Kelley Wingate Publications, Inc.

Name ______________________________ Skill: Recognizing things that go together

Draw a line to match the objects that go together.

Color the matching objects the same color.

©1995 Kelley Wingate Publications, Inc.

Name ______________________________________

Skill: Recognizing things that go together

Draw a line to match the objects that go together.
Color the matching objects the same color.

©1995 Kelley Wingate Publications, Inc.

Skill: Recognizing things that go together

Name ____________________________

Draw a line to match the objects that belong together.

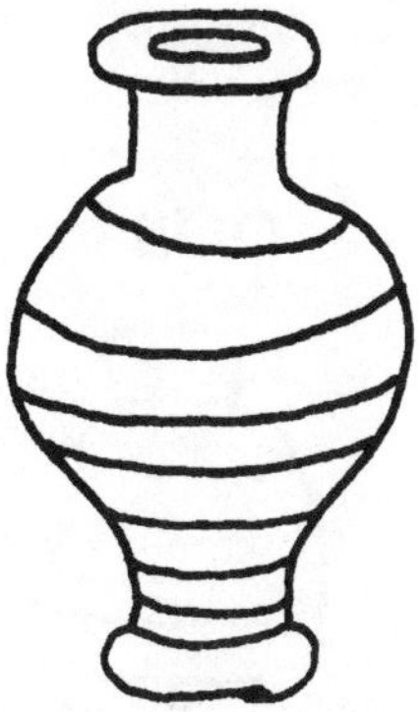

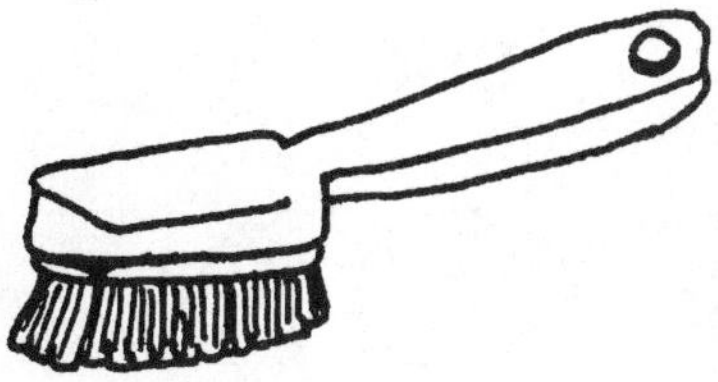

©1995 Kelley Wingate Publications, Inc.

Name ____________________ Skill: Recognizing rhyming pairs

Draw a line to match the rhyming pairs.
Color the rhyming pairs the same color.

snail

tree

bee

skirt

chair

pail

shell

bell

shirt

pair

Name________________________________ Skill: Recognizing rhyming pairs

Draw a line to match the rhyming pairs.
Color the matching pairs the same color.

whale

boat

snake

star

goat

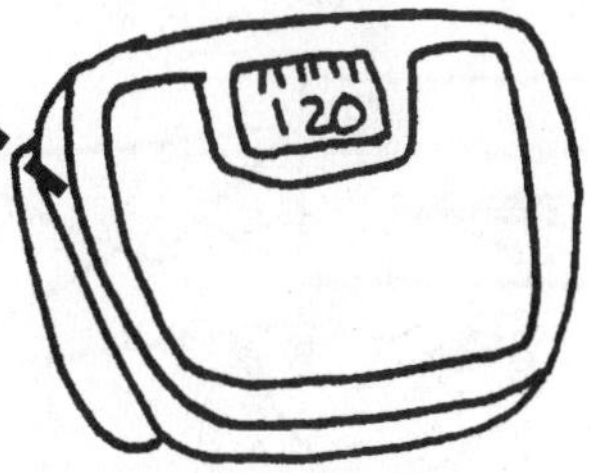

scale

car

cat

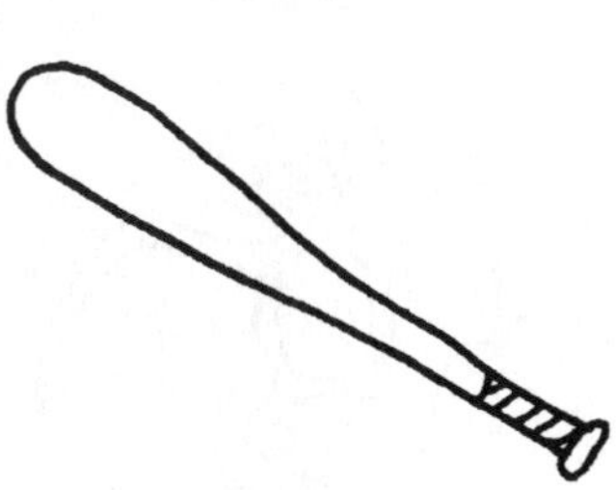

bat

cake

©1995 Kelley Wingate Publications, Inc.

Name________________________ Skill: Recognizing rhyming pairs

Draw a line to match the rhyming pairs.

frog

clock

mail

hat

pear

nail

dog

bear

sock

bat

Name________________________________ Skill: Recognizing rhyming pairs

In each row circle the two pictures that rhyme.

book

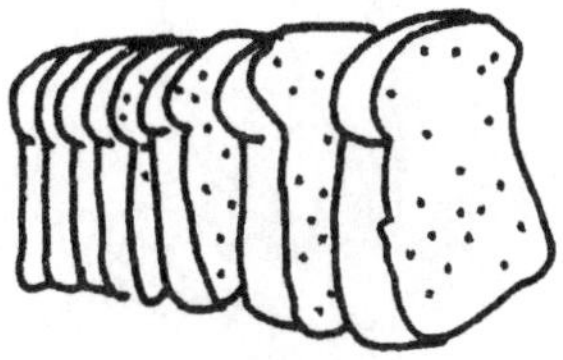
bread

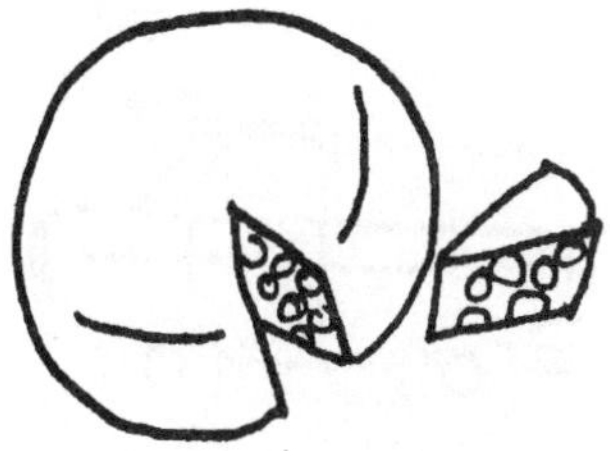
cheese

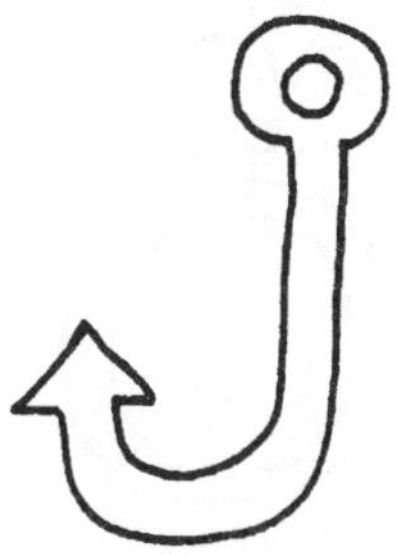
hook

glass

moon

turkey

spoon

tag

flag

vest

key

zipper

mitten

kitten

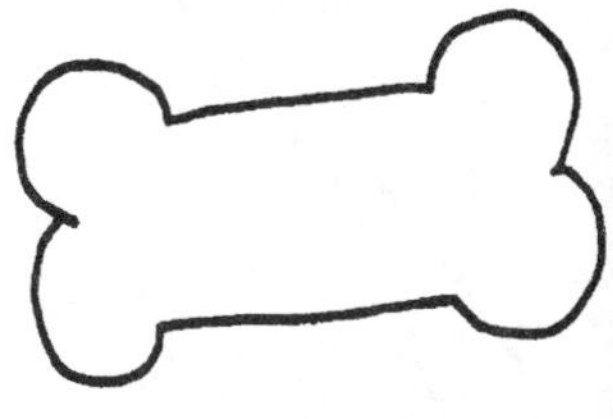
bone

©1995 Kelley Wingate Publications, Inc.

Name________________________________ Skill: Recognizing rhyming pairs

In each row circle the two pictures that rhyme.

ring

truck

bird

duck

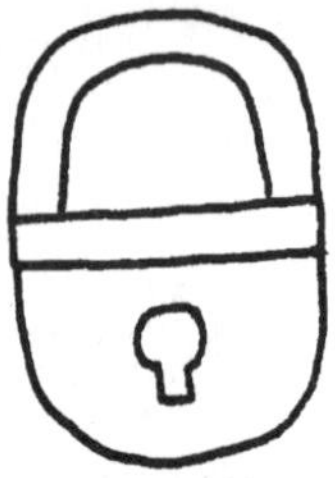
lock

egg

rock

owl

fish

cake

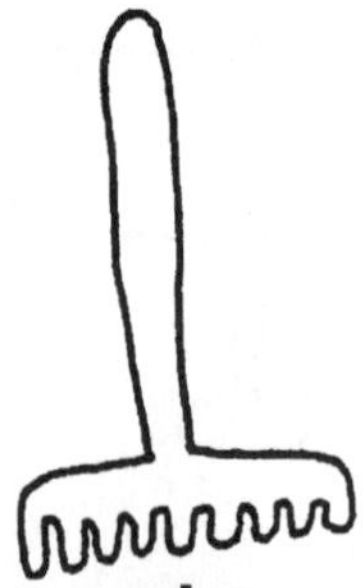
rake

heart

fork

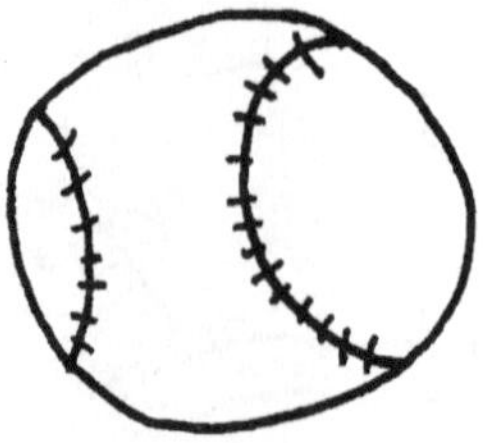
ball

bug

rug

©1995 Kelley Wingate Publications, Inc.

Name ________________________ Skill: Recognizing rhyming pairs

In each box circle the two pictures that rhyme.
Color the matching pairs.

house

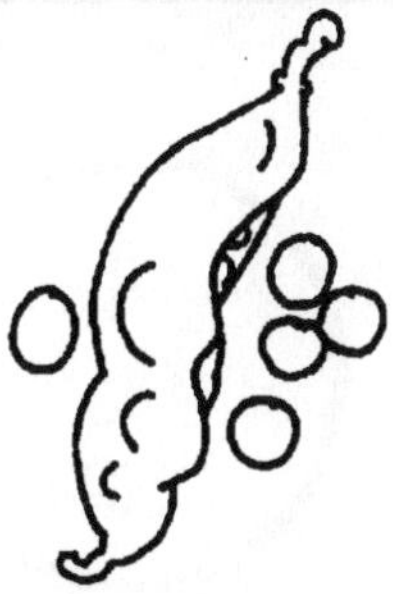
peas

mop

mouse

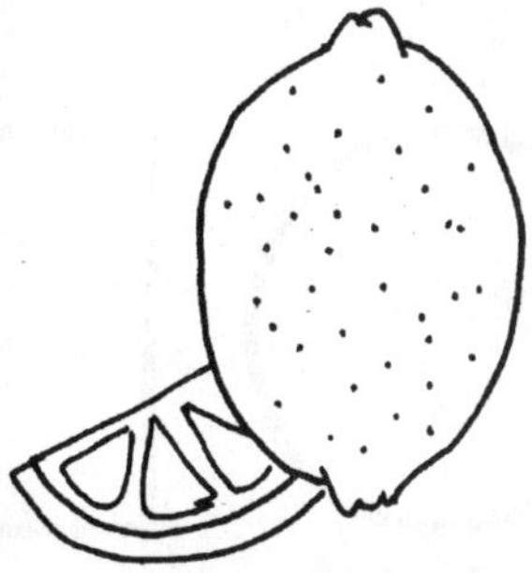
lemon

stamp

lamp

gas

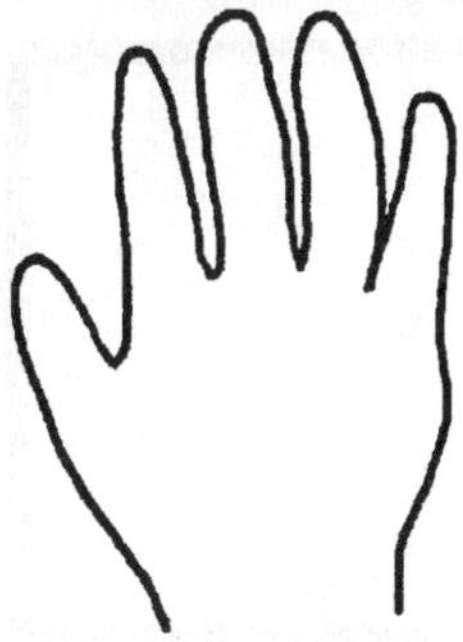
hand

nurse

bus

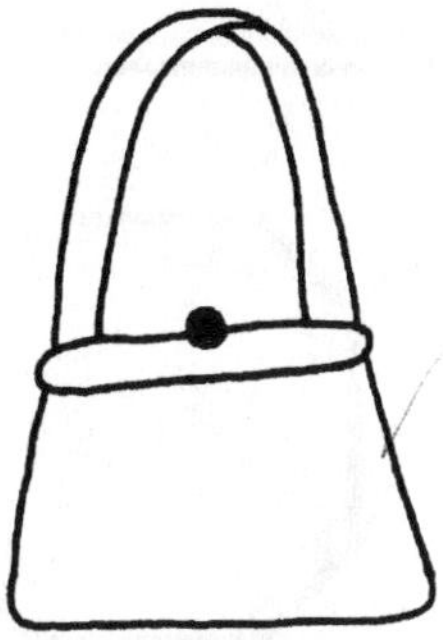
purse

bow

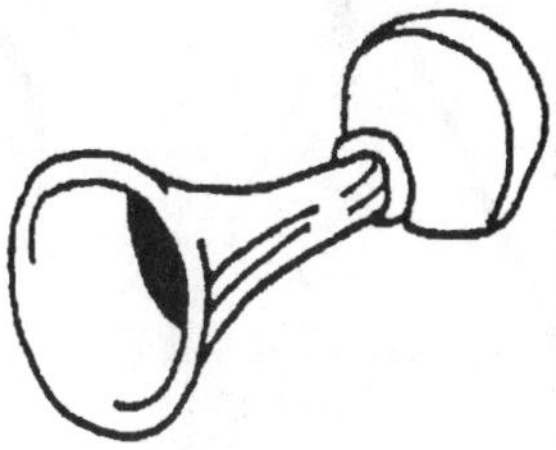
horn

hose

rose

©1995 Kelley Wingate Publications, Inc.

Name ______________________________ Skill: Recognizing what comes next

Complete each row by drawing the shape that goes next in the box.

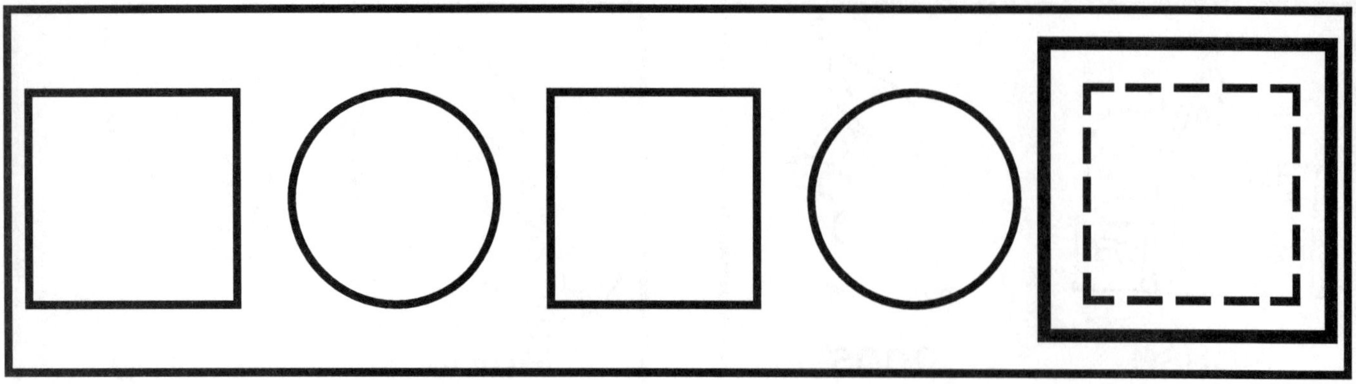

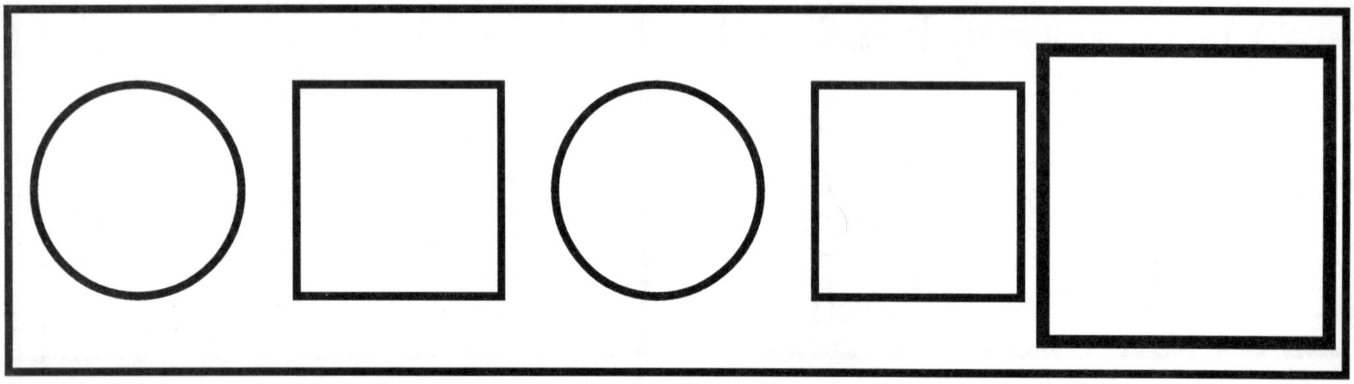

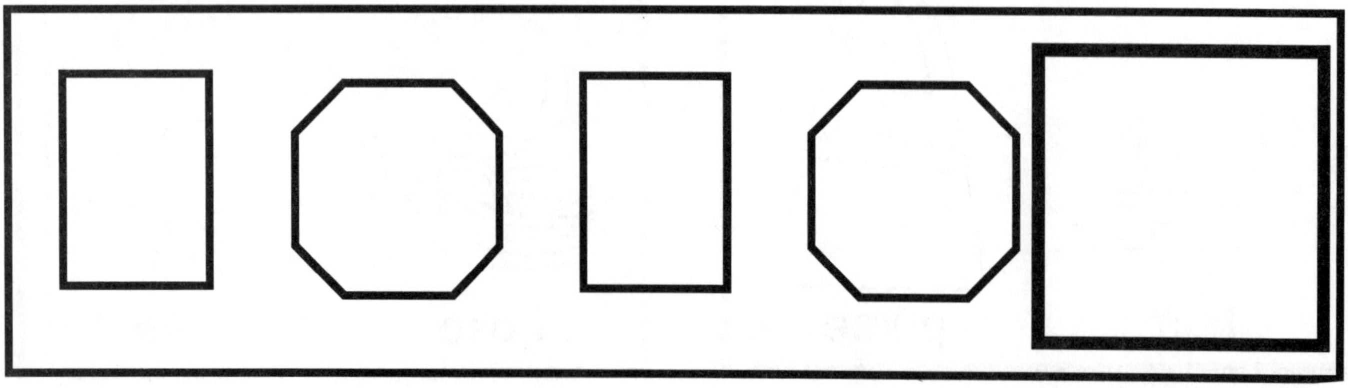

Name ____________________ Skill: Recognizing what comes next

Finish each string of beads by completing the pattern.

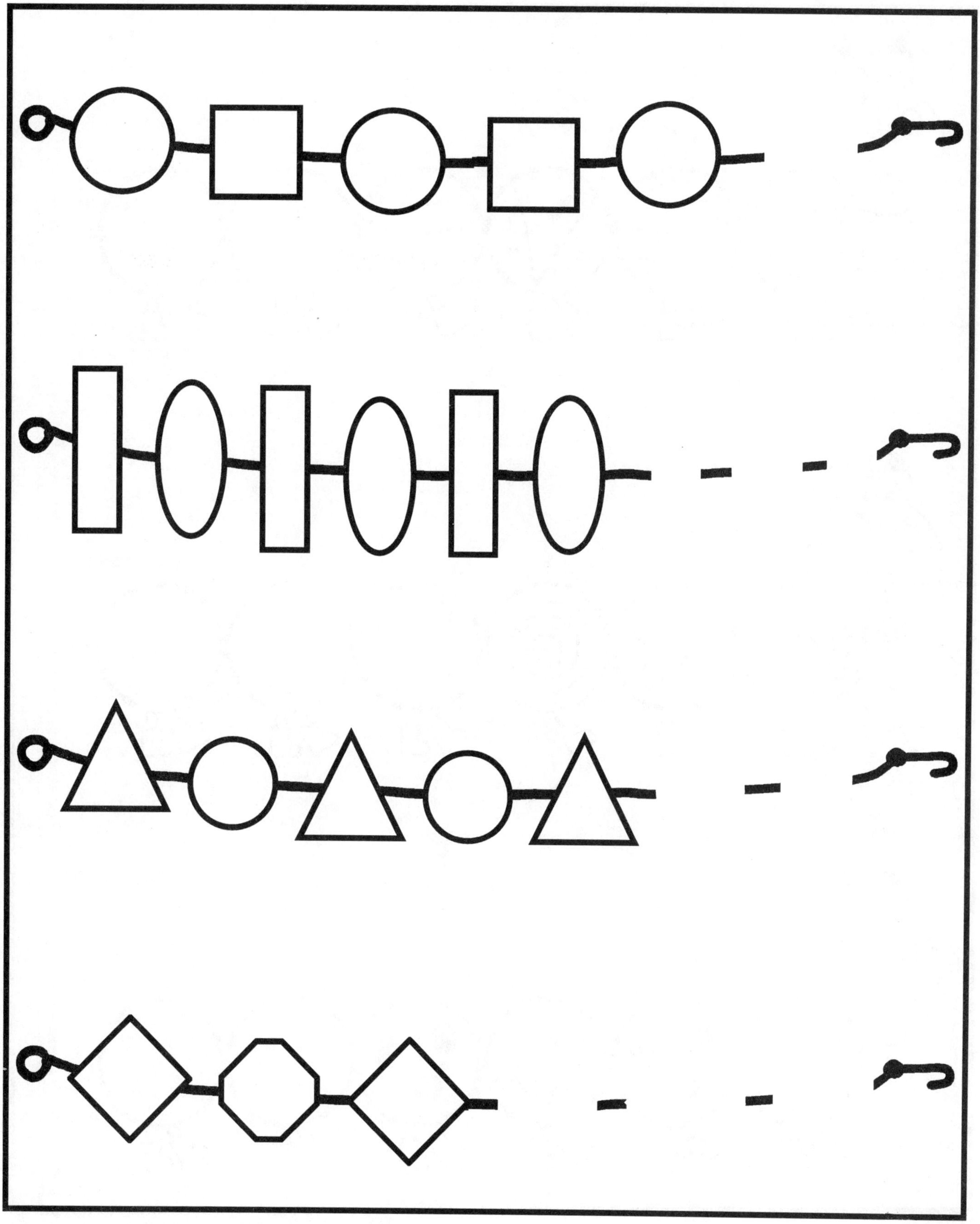

©1995 Kelley Wingate Publications, Inc.

Name ______________________ Skill: Recognizing what comes next

Fill in the blank circles to complete the pattern and finish the wacky worm.

Name ____________________

✂ Cut out the scrambled picture pieces. Paste them together to make an ice cream cone like the one below. Color the completed ice cream cone.

Name ______________________________ Skill: Sequencing

✂ Cut out the scrambled picture pieces. Paste them together to make a flamingo like the one below. Color the completed flamingo.

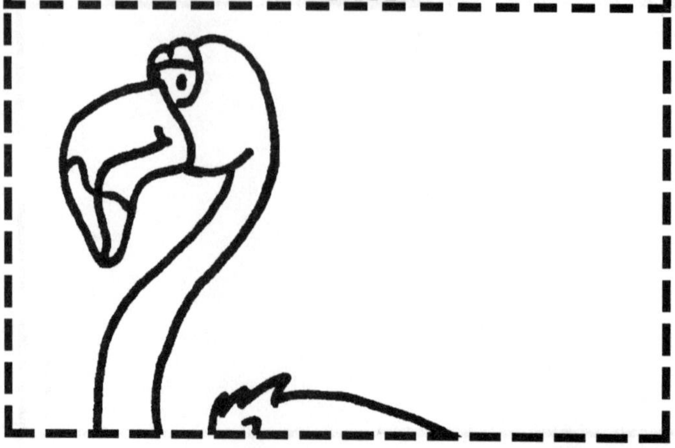

Name ____________________ Skill: Sequencing

✂ Cut out the scrambled picture pieces. Paste them together to make a giraffe like the one below. Color the completed giraffe.

©1995 Kelley Wingate Publications, Inc.

Name ______________________________ Skill: Sequencing

✂ Cut out the scrambled picture pieces. Paste them together to make a singing canary like the one below. Color the completed canary.

Name ______________________________ Skill: Sequencing

✂ Cut out the scrambled picture pieces. Paste them together to make a bear like the one below. Color the completed bear.

Name ______________________________ Skill: Learning green

Use a green crayon to color the things that are usually green.

frog

tree

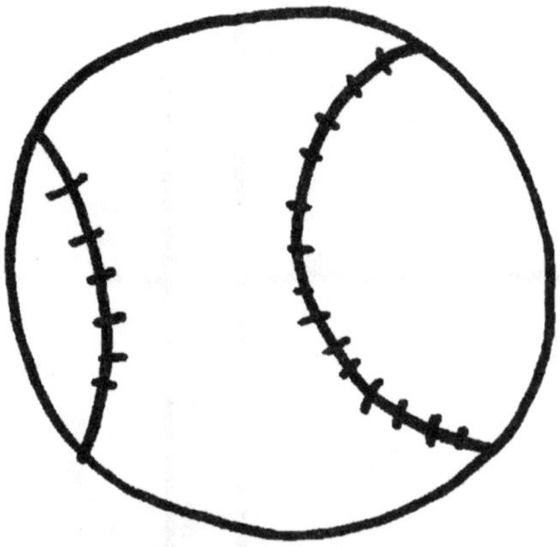

baseball

peas

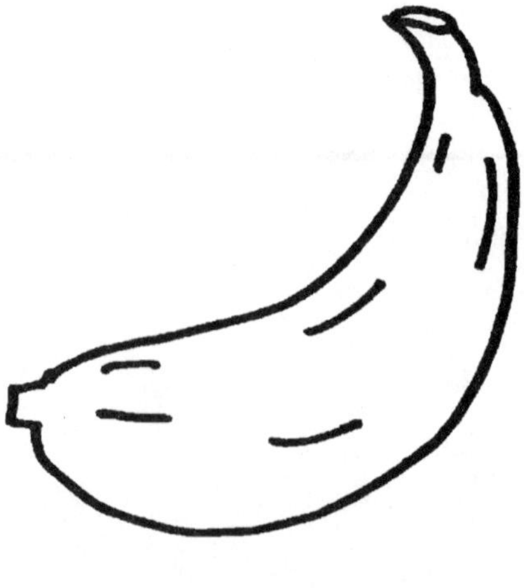

banana

©1995 Kelley Wingate Publications, Inc.

Name ______________________________ Skill: Learning yellow

Use a yellow crayon to color the things that are usually yellow.

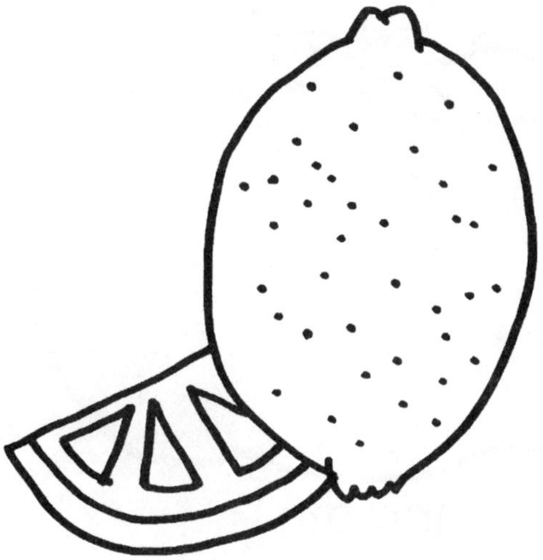
lemon

banana

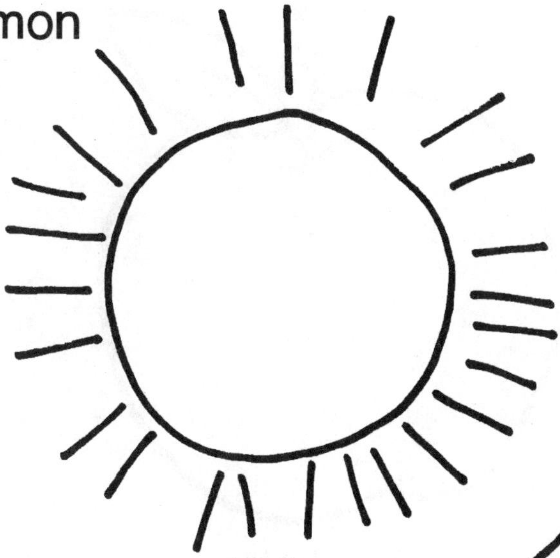
sun

frog

stop sign

©1995 Kelley Wingate Publications, Inc.

Name ______________________________ Skill: Learning red

Use a red crayon to color the things that are usually red.

whale

tomato

apple

heart

strawberry

Name ______________________________ Skill: Learning orange

Use an orange crayon to color the things that are usually orange.

pumpkin

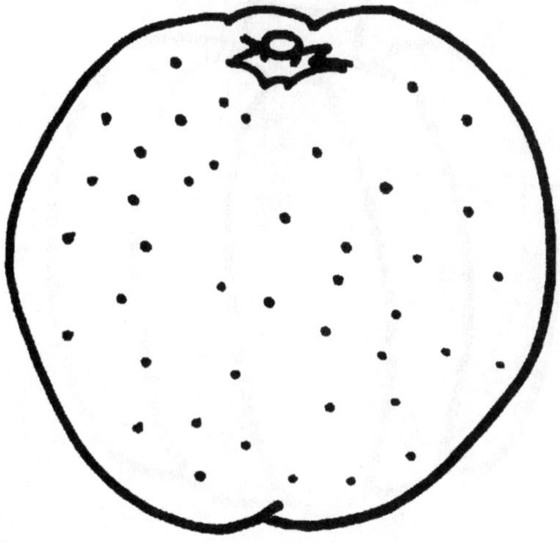

orange

carrot

heart

basketball

©1995 Kelley Wingate Publications, Inc.

Name ________________________________ Skill: Learning colors

Color each picture the correct color.

pumpkin-orange

apple-red

frog-green

corn-yellow

teddy bear-brown

Name ____________________ Skill: Learning colors

Color each picture the correct color.

elephant-gray

grapes-purple

bird-blue

flower-pink

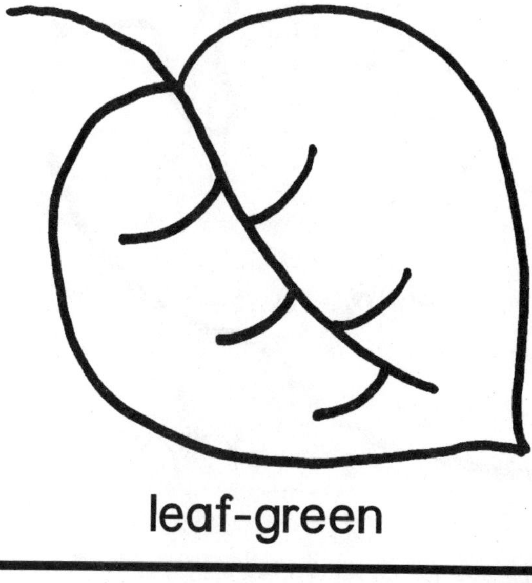

leaf-green

©1995 Kelley Wingate Publications, Inc.

Name ______________________________ Skill: Learning colors

Color each space the correct color.

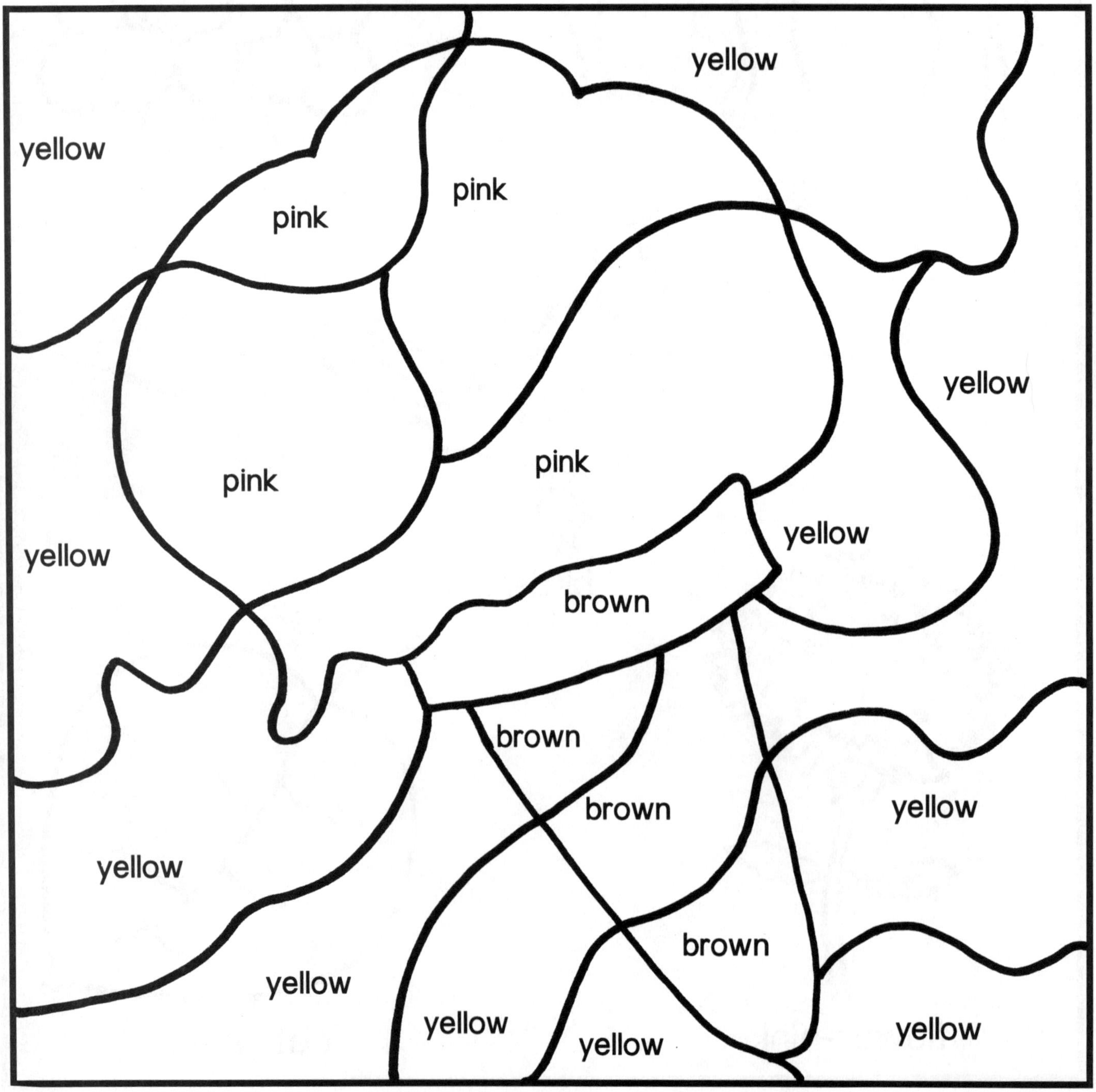

Name ____________________ Skill: Learning colors

Color each space the correct color.

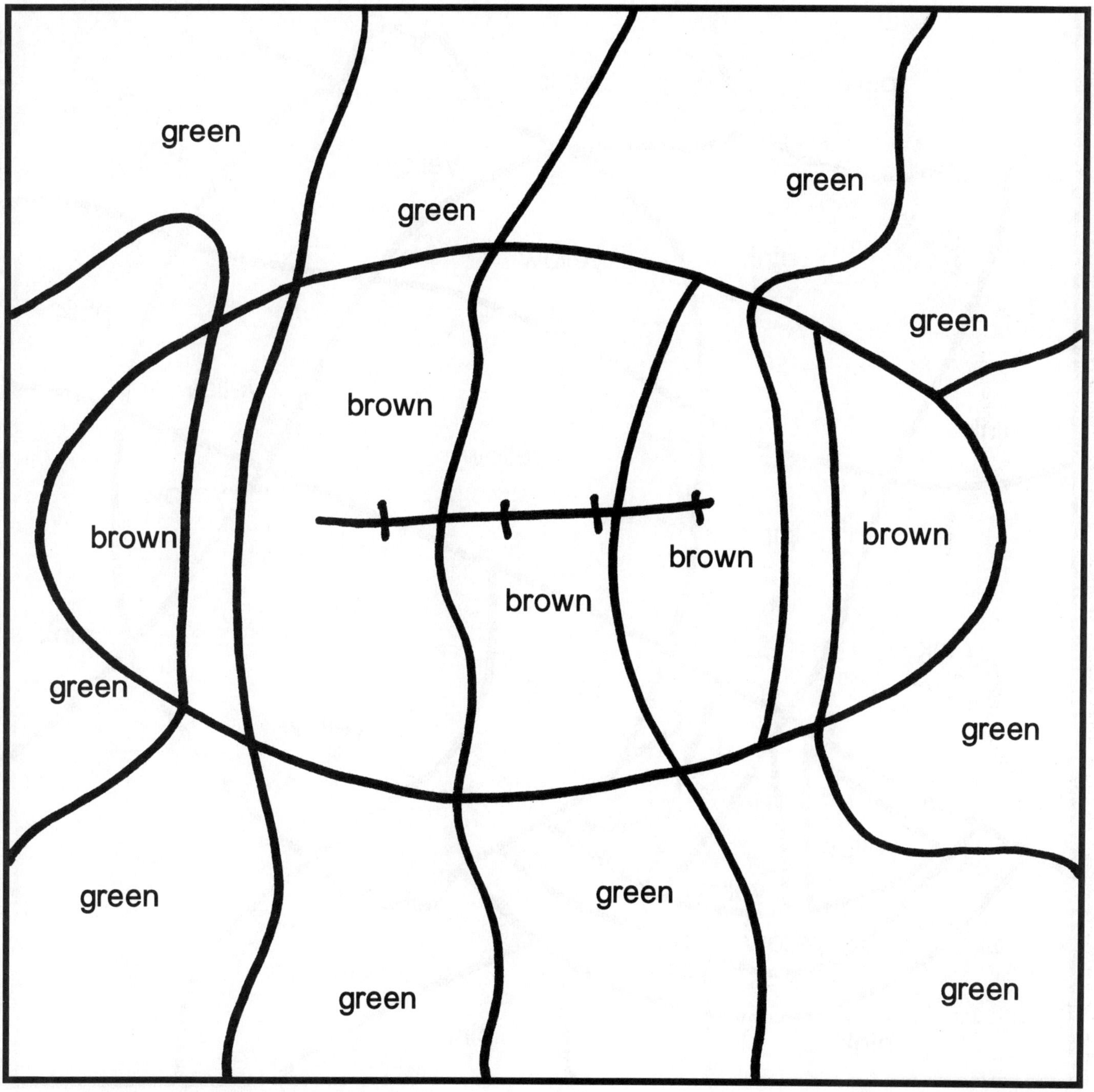

©1995 Kelley Wingate Publications, Inc.

Name ______________________________ Skill: Learning colors

Color each space the correct color.

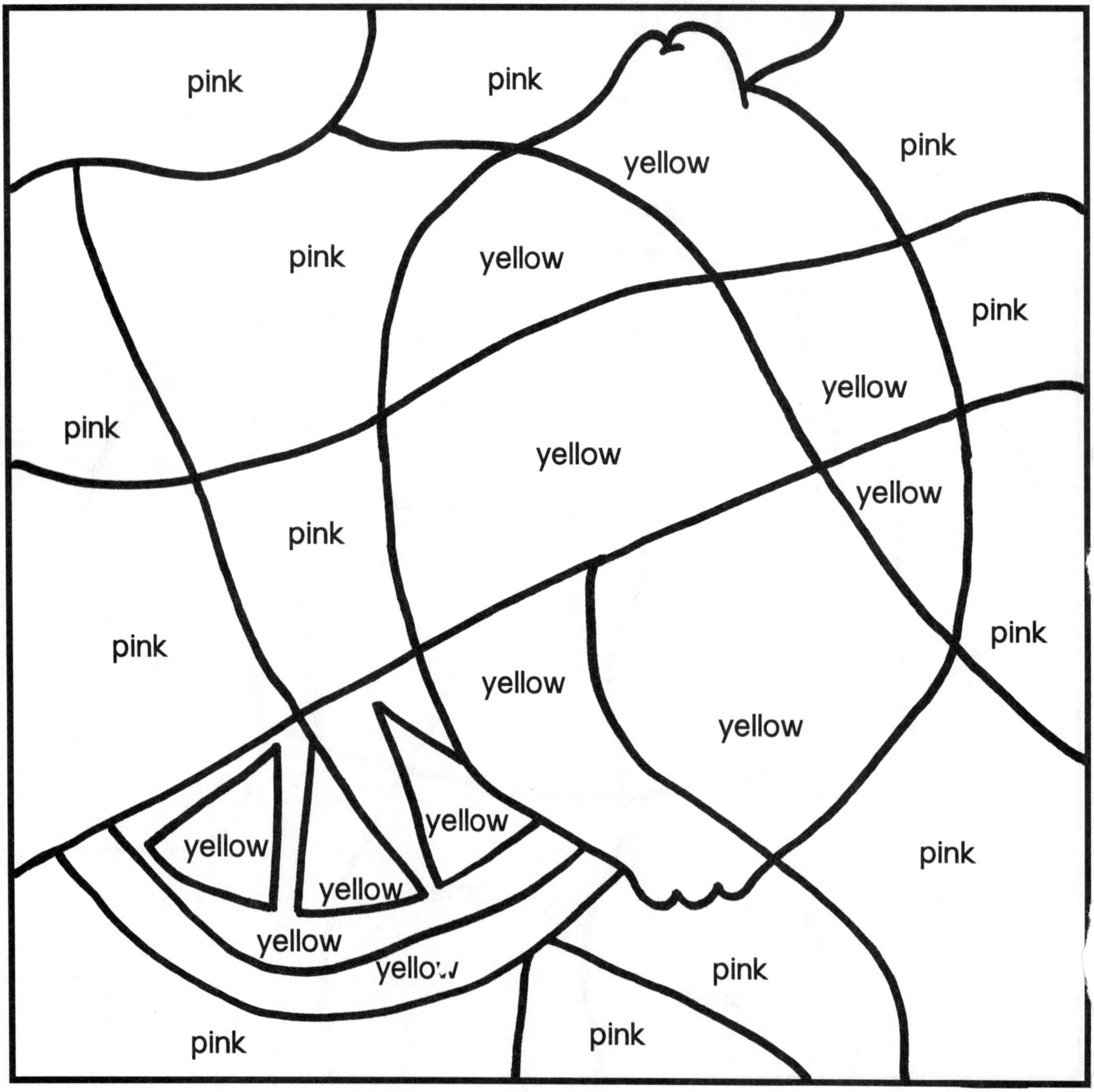

©1995 Kelley Wingate Publications, Inc.

Name ________________________________ Skill: Counting 1-5

Trace each numeral and draw a line to match it to the correct number of snowflakes.

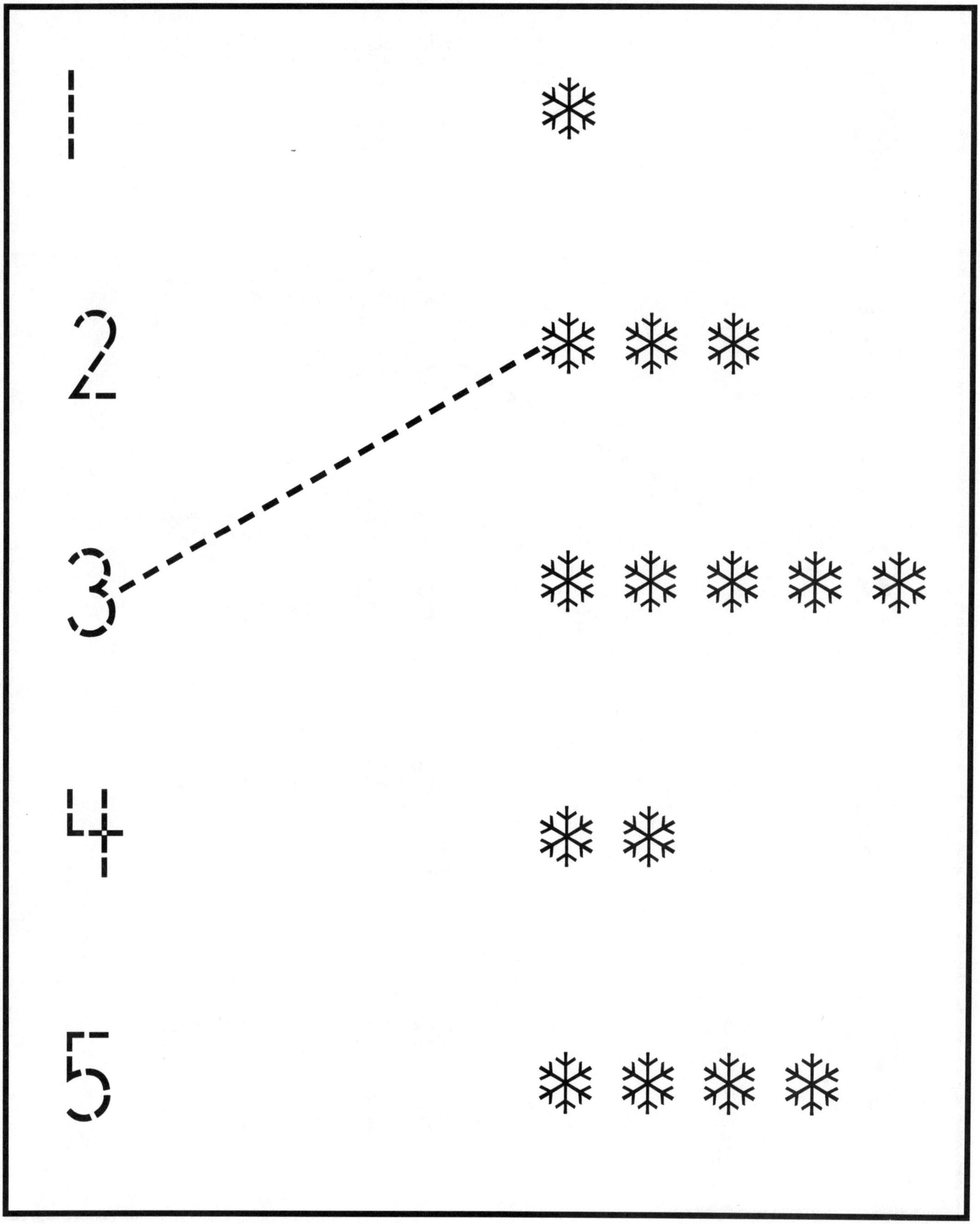

©1995 Kelley Wingate Publications, Inc.

Name ______________________________ Skill: Counting 6-10

Trace each numeral and draw a line to match it to the correct number of snowflakes.

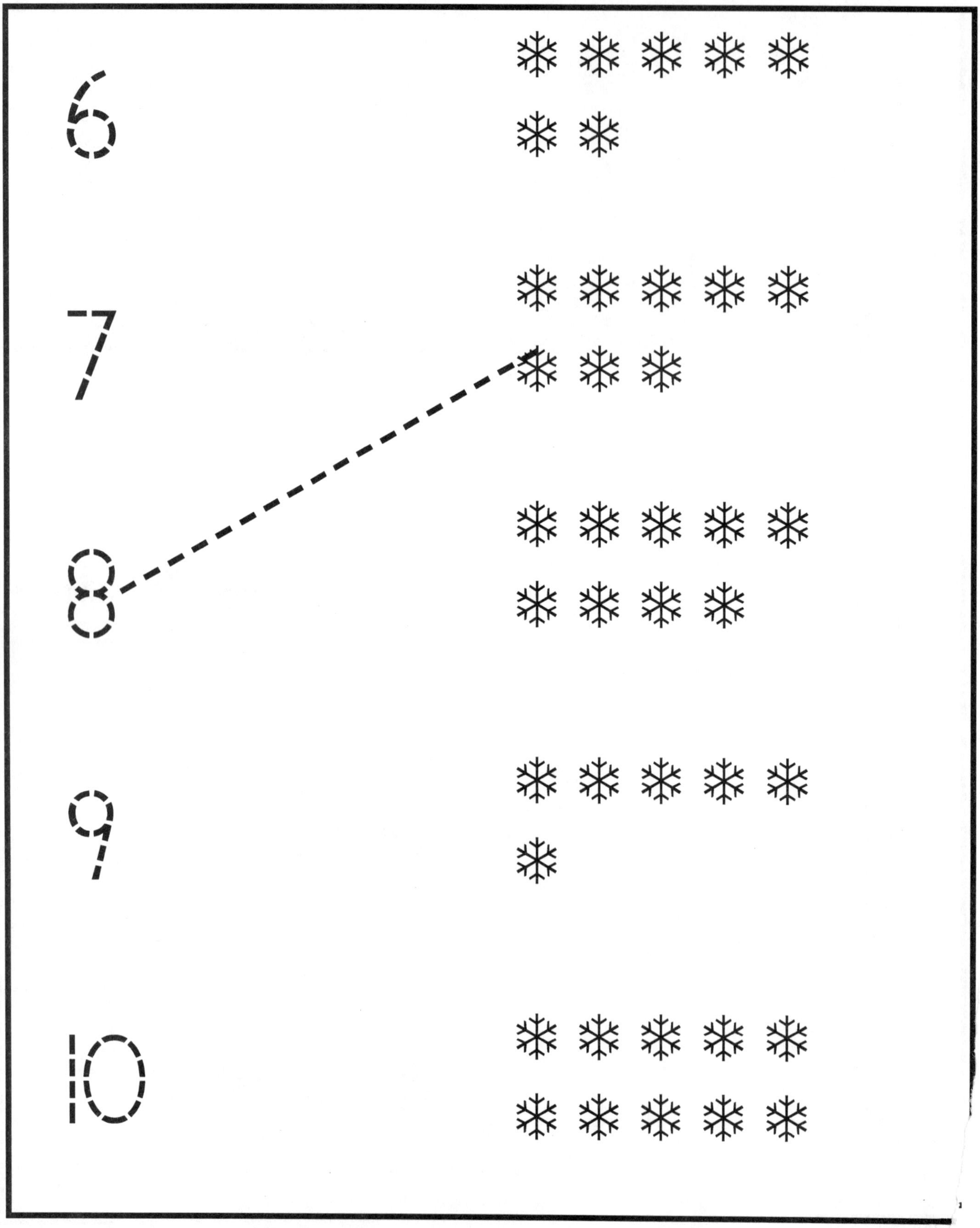

©1995 Kelley Wingate Publications, Inc.

Alphabet Award

____

receives this award for

____

Keep up the great work!

_______________________ _______________

signed date

I Know My Colors

____

receives this award for

____

Great Job!

_______________________ _______________

signed date

★ Numbers Award ★

____

receives this award for

____

Keep up the great work!

______________________ ______________

signed date

I Know My Shapes

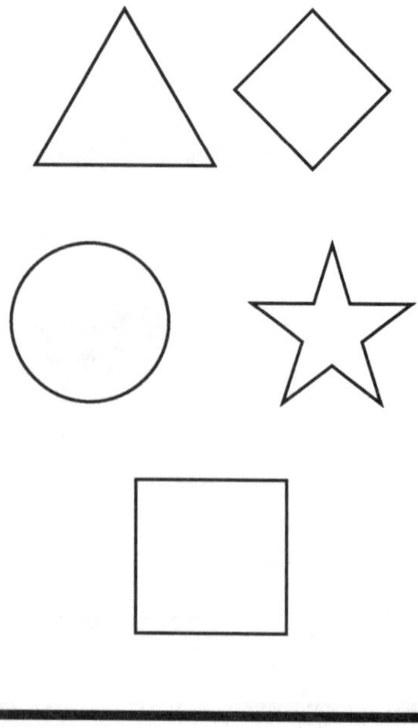

____

receives this award for

____

Great Job!

______________________ ______________

signed date

We are proud of you!

____

deserves this award for

____

Keep up the great work!

______________________ ______________________

signed date

©1995 Kelley Wingate Publications, Inc.

Alphabet, Colors, Numbers, and Shapes Certificate

This certifies that

____

knows the alphabet, colors, numbers, and shapes and is entitled to receive this certificate

Given at ______________________________

this _______ day of ________________ 19___.

Great Job!

____

Receives this award for

____

Keep up the great work!

______________ ______________

Signed Date

You Did It!

______________________ earns this award for

____

Keep Up The Great Work!

______________________________ Signed

__________ Date

Congratulations!

____

Receives this award for

____

Keep up the great work!

____________________ Signed

____________________ Date

Keep up the Great Work!

________________________ **earns this award for**

____

You are TERRIFIC!

________________________________ ____________

Signed Date

Green	Blue	Yellow	Orange
Brown	Red	Black	White

Circle Star Triangle Diamond

Oval Rectangle Heart Square

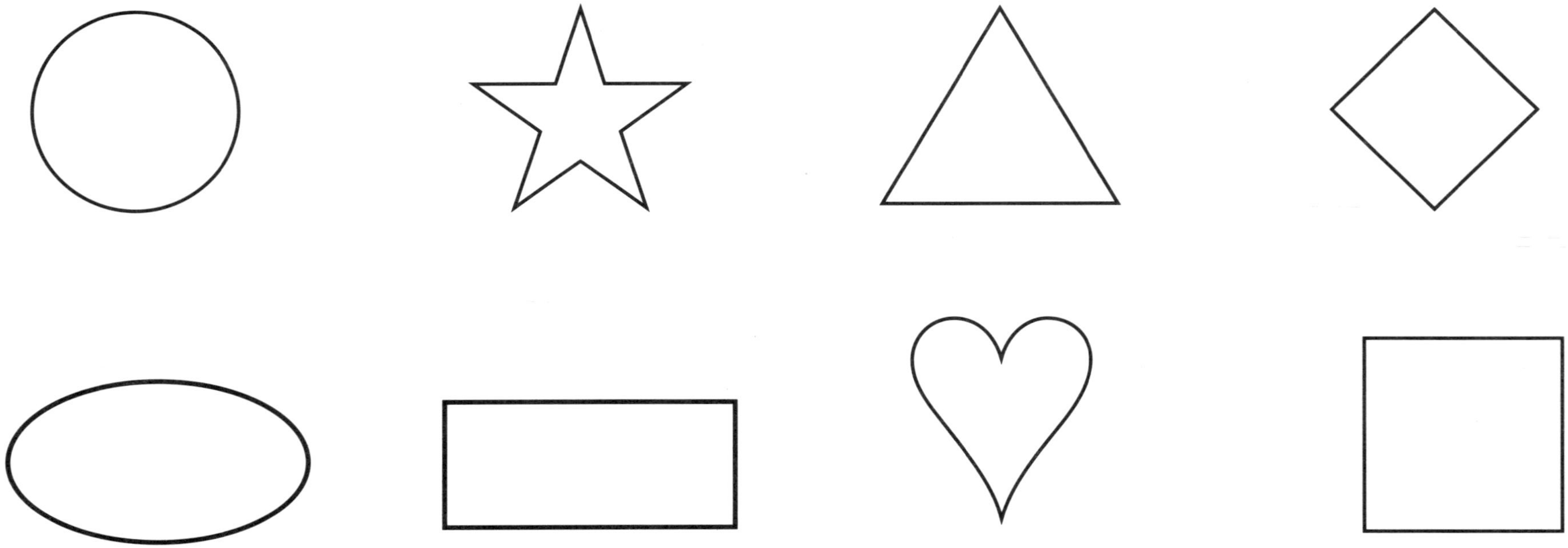

M	I	E	A
N	J	F	B
O	K	G	C
P	L	H	D

12	8	4	0
13	9	5	1
14	10	6	2
15	11	7	3

c	Y	U	Q
d	Z	V	R
e	a	W	S
f	b	X	T

28	24	20	16
29	25	21	17
30	26	22	18
31	27	23	19

s	o	k	g
t	p	l	h
u	q	m	i
v	r	n	j

80	40	36	32
90	50	37	33
100	60	38	34
+	70	39	35

nine	five	one	w
ten	six	two	x
eleven	seven	three	y
twelve	eight	four	z

thirty-seven	thirty-three	twenty-nine	$-$
thirty-eight	thirty-four	thirty	$=$
thirty-nine	thirty-five	thirty-one	$<$
forty	thirty-six	thirty-two	$>$

twenty-five	twenty-one	seventeen	thirteen
twenty-six	twenty-two	eighteen	fourteen
twenty-seven	twenty-three	nineteen	fifteen
twenty-eight	twenty-four	twenty	sixteen

eighty

forty-nine

forty-five

forty-one

ninety

fifty

forty-six

forty-two

one-hundred

sixty

forty-seven

forty-three

seventy

forty-eight

forty-four